SHOPIFY

A Beginner's Guide to Building an eCommerce Business by Dropshipping or Creating your Own Products

By Alex Greene

SHOPIFY

Table of Contents

INTRODUCTION

As soon as you need to head out for your 9-to-5 job in the morning, do you start wishing you had something better to do? Do you want to start a business on the side to supplement your income? Do you want to create a passive stream of income? Do you want to indulge in your entrepreneurial skills? If you ever had a dream to work from your home or anywhere in the world for that matter, then creating and running an online store will certainly come in handy. Also, there is no time like the present to get started on working toward this dream.

The simplest way to create an eCommerce business for yourself is by using Shopify. Shopify is an all-round eCommerce solution for businesses that wish to sell their products online. So, you don't need any massive capital or investments to start your business. All that you need is a good idea and a reliable Internet connection. Also, you don't need any technical knowledge to create an eCommerce website. If the thought of creating a website seems daunting, don't worry because you aren't alone. Plenty of people feel this way before they realize how simple Shopify is. Shopify simplifies your work, and it takes less than 20 minutes to create a skeletal framework of your e-commerce store on Shopify. Shopify is an incredible and intuitive platform that allows you to personalize your online store, sell any products you want, and accept various forms of payment while providing good customer service.

If you are looking for a simple setup and a no-hassle shopping cart experience that allows you to concentrate on your core business functions, then use Shopify. In this book, you will learn all the secrets of starting and maintaining a prosperous online retail business using Shopify. Regardless of whether you are a small or a medium scale business or are starting to think of an eCommerce store, Shopify offers a variety of features and benefits. This is ready to use an eCommerce platform. It's specially created for entrepreneurs who aren't well versed in web designing and development. Shopify essentially makes the entire online store setup an incredibly easy experience without compromising on the functionality you would expect from a professional eCommerce platform.

In this book, you will learn about Shopify, the benefits it offers and how to set up an eCommerce store with success. You will also learn about selecting the right theme for the Shopify store, designing the website, various Shopify applications, setting up an email list, and marketing the store online. The Shopify store you start can be based on the model of drop-shipping or private labeling. You will learn in detail about these two business models. Once you carefully go through all the information given in this book, you will feel confident about starting your own eCommerce store on Shopify.

So, are you eager to learn more about all this? If yes, then let's get started immediately.

CHAPTER ONE

WHY USE SHOPIFY?

Shopify is one of the most popular digital retailing platforms available these days. The minute you decide to open an online store and eCommerce store, there are a variety of shopping cart platforms to choose from. So, what is Shopify?

Tobias Lutke created Shopify out of sheer necessity. He required an eCommerce platform that offers sufficient flexibility to be easily integrated with various other services. This idea prompted him to work with Scott Lake to develop an e-commerce platform.

Initially, Tobias was keen on creating a platform that helped him to sell his snowboards to an online audience. However, after a while, he wanted to help various other online entrepreneurs like himself by selling their products online. It is the primary motivation that leads to the creation of Shopify.

Lutke and Scott were primarily focused on creating an e-commerce platform that offered plenty of flexibility and was easy to use. Shopify was launched in 2006, and there was no turning back. After struggling for two years, both the creators came up with a new team to turn Shopify into the digital platform that we all know and love today. By 2008, Shopify managed to register its first profits, and it began to gather recognition as an ideal eCommerce platform slowly. Shopify managed to secure an additional $ 7 million funding in 2010 and $15 million funding than 2011.

A humble platform that started out with the idea of selling snowboards online soon developed into a vast eCommerce platform with over 500,000 registered eCommerce stores. Also, this platform isn't just used by small businesses, but also various big and popular brands such as Red Bull, Angry Birds, 50 Cent, and Foo Fighters. It is believed that by 2017, Shopify managed to transact over $ 40 billion in merchandise as sales from all its stores. Shopify is an eCommerce solution that allows store owners to set up their online stores. While using Shopify, you don't have to worry about any issues associated with server maintenance, hosting, or brand representation to the customers. The various auxiliary applications available can be readily used on Shopify and will help address all these issues.

Shopify offers plenty of customization options ranging from inventory management, tracking customer use, managing the online store, or even customer contact. The primary aim of Shopify is to help potential entrepreneurs and online store owners to set up their eCommerce stores even if they have no technical knowledge or background on coding. All the features Shopify offers are not only customizable but incredibly easy to use too. So, even if you have absolutely no technical skills whatsoever, you can easily establish your online store to sell products produced by others or your own products. The different challenges associated with designing and launching an eCommerce store are eliminated by using Shopify as the hosting platform.

Benefits of Using Shopify

Now that you are aware of what Shopify is about to let's look at the different benefits it offers.

Easy to Use

Plenty of entrepreneurs have incredible ideas, but not everyone is tech-savvy. Such entrepreneurs might harbor fears about starting their own eCommerce stores because of all the problems they might run into due to their lack of technical knowledge. While using Shopify, you don't have to worry about understanding or having any previous knowledge about coding. From servers to hosting, everything is taken care of by Shopify. All you need is a name or brand free online shop and the products you wish to sell.

Shopify provides plenty of tutorials you can go through before setting up your online store. Once you are aware of how it works, open the Shopify website, create an account, and register your store. As soon as this step is completed, all that's left to do is customize the store, upload your product images, and start using it as a seller. Using Shopify is incredibly easy. After the product has been uploaded, you can customize the color schemes, the theme of the store, add titles to the images, and even edit the product descriptions. All the inventory you hold can be easily managed and monitored through the Shopify dashboard. You can also use it to track the sales orders, manage all the transactions, and even create offers for your customers. Pretty much anything that you can think of for establishing and running a successful online store is taken care of by Shopify.

Security and Reliability

Security matters in all aspects of your life, and an online store is not an exception. We live in a technology-dominated world where digitization has become the norm of different aspects of our lives. With the rise in technology, there's also an increase in cyber threats. So, as an online store owner, you might be worried about the security and reliability of the hosting service, especially in the wake of an increase in cybercrimes such as hacking. Your online store will contain plenty of sensitive information that is not just yours, but also the valuable information of your customer. Therefore, security and reliability will be critical for establishing a successful online store.

Its reliable hosting system, coupled with the strong security it offers, makes Shopify quite endearing to eCommerce store owners. Once these issues are taken care of, you can concentrate all your resources on growing and expanding your business. Also, all online stores invariably end up handling sensitive customer information like their personal details and even the details of the debit or credit cards. Therefore, you must guarantee not only the security of your own information but also the information your customers provide while using your Shopify store. Handling credit card information and bank details is an important aspect of online business, and assuring security is your responsibility. Apart from all this, the customers also expect the store to be online all of the time and offer fast page loading speeds. With Shopify, all that's left to you to do is concentrate on selling your products without worrying about the nitty-gritty of the online store.

Convenient Mobile Access

Long gone are the days when using the Internet was restricted to bulky desktops. These days, most of the Internet users access it with their smartphones.

Therefore, plenty of websites are being designed such that they are equally responsive to smaller and larger screens. Since most people are accessing the Internet via their phones, your website must be mobile-friendly. If your potential customers cannot easily access your website, then you will start losing more of your business to other competitors present in the niche.

Ensuring that the website is mobile-friendly improves the overall customer experience and might eventually lead to an increase in your overall sales. If you're worried about how your website can be optimized for a smaller screen like mobile phones, then you have nothing to worry about. Why not? Well, Shopify does it all for you. According to any of your requirements for website responsiveness, Shopify will keep updating the website to keep up with the new updates. This simple service offered by Shopify is in sync with the platform's goal of managing all the technical aspects involved in managing the online store. Once all these things are taken care of, all that you are required to do is concentrate on maximizing your sales.

Easy App Installation

It's not just about the website is easily accessed or optimized for mobile use, but your online store will also need a mobile application. Since a lot of people use their phones for online shopping, the mobile app allows your potential customers to access your site directly. Also, it gives you the option of managing your Shopify store on the go. So, regardless of whether you are at home or on vacation, you can easily track your orders, edit, or update them, and also manage the online store through your phone using the app.

Not just mobile applications, there are various other applications quite similar to plug-ins, you can install and activate on the online store for improving the overall flexibility. There are several apps available on Shopify that are designed to help you do various things on the online store essentially. There are apps that you can install, which allow the customers to leave a review or use an app that allows you to track any inquiries you receive from the customers. By installing and activating all these applications, it gives your website the desired flexibility for improving the overall customer experience.

Payment Gateways

As an online retailer, opting for a secure and reliable payment gateway is quite important. The payment gateway you choose must provide the customers with a variety of payment options. A payment gateway is usually a critical issue for various self-hosted eCommerce websites, but when it comes to Shopify, it is not an issue. Setting up the payment gateway is quite easy while using Shopify. The stripe payment option offered by Shopify enables you and your customers to make various transactions on your eCommerce website without incurring any extra fees. A merchant account isn't compulsory to use the stripe services.

Even if your customers don't have a credit card, they can use other payment gateways, like PayPal, for transacts on your Shopify eCommerce store. Did you know your Shopify store name would appear on your customer's statement whenever they make a transaction with your business? This is a great opportunity to work on your branding to increase brand loyalty subtly.

Good Visuals

Unlike the bricks and mortar store, your customers cannot visit your store at its physical location. They cannot see the products in real life or the way your store looks. So, the website you create for the eCommerce store or the online layout is as important as the physical storefront of a conventional store. If you wish to become a successful eCommerce business store owner, then the store must be visually appealing to your target audience.

Whenever someone visits your eCommerce store, they will see the various images or pictures used for displaying your products. Therefore, it's quintessential to make the eCommerce store look visually appealing. Shopify thoroughly understands the importance of making an online store visually appealing. Therefore, they offer a variety of layouts and themes to create a professional yet visually attractive store. Shopify also offers a variety of customization options. So, each store on Shopify can be as unique, special, different, and specific as you wanted to be. You can also change or edit the product descriptions, images, and even the titles.

Affordable

Creating an eCommerce site by hiring the services of a web developer can cost anywhere between $ 3000 and $ 5000. This is a significant expenditure, especially when it comes to small businesses and startups. Any entrepreneur aims to minimize the costs of operation while maximizing the returns. Because of its affordable pricing structure, Shopify has become a popular option among online retailers across the globe. Shopify offers a subscription model, where you pay a predetermined monthly fee for using the platform. When compared to all the benefits you stand to gain from Shopify, the costs involved are quite low.

Marketing Options

Setting up an online store doesn't mean customers will start flowing in. So, you need to concentrate on marketing your business. One of the marketing techniques you cannot afford to overlook is optimizing the online store for search engines. It is known as search engine optimization (SEO). It ensures that your website is easily found by anyone looking for specific keywords associated with your products. Shopify helps enhance the ability to develop effective landing pages for your marketing campaigns. This marketing feature effectively distinguishes Shopify from various other online shopping carts and eCommerce platforms. Shopify also allows you to customize the Meta and title tags for better search engine optimization.

Recovering Abandoned Carts

Not all those who browse through your website need to end up making a purchase. Most visitors often browse through the website, build a cart, and then abandon it without completing the purchase. Shopify has a rather interesting feature that allows eCommerce store owners to send email reminders to all those visitors who didn't complete their purchases or who have abandoned their carts. By doing this, you can increase your overall conversion rate. At times, all it takes is a gentle reminder to nudge a potential buyer to become a paying customer.

Good Customer Support

An important benefit offered by Shopify is the customer service it provides. Shopify offers a variety of tutorial videos that allow you to understand how to use the platform, tips for getting started, and basic troubleshooting techniques. Also, they offer 24/7 customer support. Regardless of the time of the day, you can always reach out to someone at Shopify if you need any help or support.

After going through all the different benefits Shopify offers, you might be quite excited to build your online store!

Shopify vs. WordPress

A common question a lot of entrepreneurs have while creating an e-commerce store is whether they should use Shopify or WordPress. What platform should you opt for? Are there any fees payable? Can I sell physical products, or is it only for information products? Can I sell private labeled items? Can I drop-ship? Well, do these questions sound familiar to you? If you are considering opening up an e-commerce store, then you have probably asked these questions.

In this section, let us look at what WordPress is, the times when Shopify is a better option than WordPress, and the reasons why you should consider using Shopify. WordPress has always been incredibly popular. In the previous sections, you were introduced to what Shopify is about, and the different benefits it offers. WordPress is a versatile platform, and you can use it to make your website easily available and accessible to the rest of the world. However, an e-commerce store is quite different from a regular blog or a news publishing website. WordPress is all about content, and most of this content is published with the intent of being consumed for free or at a minimal charge. By using WordPress, you can publish videos, pictures, blogs, etc. Still, its basic principle is that all this content will be available to anyone who stumbles upon the specific URL.

If you take a moment to think about it, an e-commerce store is quite different. Whatever an e-commerce website platform offers is secured behind a paywall. The entire site needs to be careful when dealing with important data, such as the customer's credit card or personal information. The website must be secure, and it should be capable of handling, processing, and delivering all the orders that it receives. Simply put, when compared to regular publishing platforms, an e-commerce store is quite different. So, it is time we all accepted the simple fact that WordPress isn't always the answer. If you wish to launch an e-commerce website, then you need a hosting platform that caters specifically to e-commerce stores.

So, what is the difference between Shopify and WordPress?

The one factor that differentiates Shopify from WordPress is that the former is an Internet service or tool while the latter is a software that needs to be installed. If you wish to use Shopify, then you merely need to visit their official website- Shopify.com, to create and register your profile. Once you complete the registration, quickly set up your profile, and you can start building your e-commerce store.

If you want to start using WordPress, then there are a couple more steps you must follow. The first step is to purchase a domain and a web hosting profile that allows you to install the default version of WordPress. The next step is to select a theme and design for the website and install a couple of plug-ins for social media integration, SEO, and so on. Once all this is in place, you should opt for a plug-in that provides all the e-commerce features not provided by WordPress, such as WooCommerce. The final step is to complete the configuration process of the e-commerce store. By including details, such as the payment gateway integration, product details, store details, and so on.

Another factor you must weigh up when deciding about using Shopify or WordPress is the customer support available. Shopify provides a 24/7 customer support system that you can use if you run into any trouble. On the other hand, WordPress doesn't provide any such service. Here is a simple example of putting things into perspective. Using Shopify is like visiting an IKEA store and purchasing a bookshelf. Once you are home, you merely need to assemble the bookshelf, and that's about it. Now, using WordPress is similar to visiting a hardware store, purchasing the planks, glue, nails, tools, any other things you require, and then coming home to build the bookshelf from scratch.

Shopify is the one-stop e-commerce solution you can use to easily build an e-commerce website. You can do all this without any technical knowledge, coding skills, and without hiring any professionals. The monthly fees payable for Shopify can range from $9 to $2000. You can sell any goods or services, including both physical and digital ones on Shopify. You can also use it as a drop-shipping platform. Shopify offers more than 100 online store designs, and every new website created on it gets a custom subdomain free of cost. This platform also offers 24/7 customer support.

You can use WordPress to build a website too. However, to do this, you should be able to handle technical setup such as installing software, themes, plug-ins, and an e-commerce plug-in to get started on all your online store operations. If you want to use WordPress effectively, you must have some website building knowledge and skills. According to the level of customization you want from the e-commerce store, your design and coding skills will differ. The software you use for WordPress is available free of charge, but to use it, you must sign up for a web host and purchase a domain name. The monthly cost using WordPress can be as low as $5. This platform offers plenty of content management features and thousands of free and paid themes to choose from. WordPress doesn't have any dedicated customer support, but it does have an extremely helpful community.

When is Shopify better than WordPress? Shopify offers tailor-made e-commerce solutions that are ideal for anyone who has absolutely no idea about coding or building a website. As long as you have a good business and a product idea in mind, you can leverage Shopify to build an e-commerce store without any hassle. One of the major benefits of using Shopify is that you can set up your online store within a couple of minutes, and once a store is up and running, you can open the store for business. It's not just coding or building the website, but you also don't have to worry about various other aspects of running an e-commerce store such as managing the inventory, shipping, or the taxes. Also, Shopify is an extremely affordable option.

CHAPTER TWO

HOW TO SET UP SHOPIFY STORE

In this section, let us look in detail at all the different steps you must go through to set up an e-commerce store on Shopify.

Step 1: Signing Up

The first step to creating a Shopify e-commerce store is to sign up with Shopify. To do this, visit the official Shopify website and click on the signup form to create an account. Don't forget to click on the "start free trial" button after entering all the required details. Keep in mind that the store name you opt for needs to be unique, or Shopify will prompt you to choose something else. After you enter the email address, you'll be asked to fill out a couple of other personal details like your name, country, address, contact number, alternate email address, and so on. You will also be asked questions about the products you wish to sell, whether you have the said products, and what you want to sell. If you are

16

just going through Shopify to understand how it works, then opt for the, "I'm just playing around" option in the drop-down menu of, "Do you have products?" And select "I am not sure," in the section that asks, "What will you sell?" Once you are satisfied with your answers and have completed all the fields, click on "I am done" to complete the signup process.

Step 2: Log In

Once you have completed the signup process, you can either log out or continue. If you are logged out, log in once again and go toward the store admin screen. Once at the store admin screen, it is time to customize the store, upload products, and set up different forms of payment and shipping.

Step 3: Configuration

Let us look in detail at the different settings that you need to configure while setting up the store. Here are the different steps you must follow while configuring the store to meet your requirements.

Click on the settings menu and select general options.

There are a couple of general details that you can update or change, such as the store details, standards and formats, store currency, and the store address. In the store details, the different information you might have to provide includes an email address to receive any support from Shopify, the store name, and a customer email that all potential customers will see whenever they receive an email from your store. Don't forget to add the legal name of the business, the street address, and a phone number. There are various standards and formats available to choose from. You must carefully select the unit system, the default weight unit, and the time zone. Apart from all this, please select the right store currency. Depending on your country of operation, the store currency will differ.

Click on PowerSettings Payment providers

Configuring the payment method or the mode of payment is quite important. The first step is to set up your Shopify payments, then activate a third-party payment provider. You can also activate another method or alternative method of payment. Apart from this, don't forget to activate a manual payment method as well. Ensure that the payment authorization settings are secure and easy to remember.

Settings Shipping

As the name suggests, on this page in the settings menu, you can add or edit information about shipping origin, shipping rates, size and weight of packages, or even enable third-party fulfillment services. Shipping origin is the address used to calculate the overall shipping rate. Depending on the shipping zones and corresponding shipping rates, you can set specific shipping rates at the checkout. To calculate the shipping costs, don't forget to consider the size and weight of the packages that have to be shipped.

Settings Checkout

An important part of a well-functioning e-commerce website is the checkout page. On the checkout page, you can make changes to the customer account, customer contact, order processing, email marketing, checkout, language, and all the other policies associated with your e-commerce store. In customer accounts, you have the option to choose whether a customer must create an account before he can checkout or not. Customer contact essentially offers the choice of whether customers need to provide a specific phone number or their email address before checking out. It also gives you the option to choose any contact method the customers can use to receive shipping updates. Customer forms allow you to decide whether you want to collect any other additional information from the customer before they checkout or not.

In order processing, different details about the checkout process, such as the information on the checkout page, order fulfillment, billing address, and the shipping address, will be mentioned. For the sake of email marketing, you can offer a chance for your customers to sign up or subscribe to your email marketing campaigns.

Don't forget to check the language for the checkout page. Apart from that, there are various policies, and you need to fill out the checkout page with details such as refund policy, terms of service, and the privacy policy.

Settings Notifications

This page essentially offers different notification settings like shipping notifications, customer notifications, and order notifications. The customer notifications are for any orders processed on your e-commerce stores, such as the information about invoices, order cancellations, order confirmations, order refunds, and abandoned shopping carts. The different shipping notifications include shipping update, fulfillment request, shipment or delivery, shipping confirmation, and shipping delivered. So, you have complete power to determine the kind of notifications you want or don't want to receive. When all the notification systems are in place, it helps ensure that your business is on the right track.

Settings Taxes

If you don't want to get into any legal trouble, then ensure that your store has all the necessary permissions and is paying all its taxes on time. Depending on the existing taxation policies in the country or the state the store is located in, the tax rates will differ.

Settings Sales

Managing your sales channels is quintessential for any e-commerce store owner. By using this option, you can easily manage or add sales channels to your existing e-commerce store. Sales channels help you to sell online through social networks, on mobile applications, or even in person.

Settings Files

Use this option for uploading videos, images, or any other documents. You can also manage all the files you upload using this setting.

Settings Billings

As the name suggests, this section essentially deals with all the billing associated with your Shopify store. Billing information provides information about all the invoices that are paid for using any of the chosen payment methods available on the website. You can also add a credit card to pay other invoices you have on this platform. To understand the overview of all the fees and payouts, such as the Shopify subscriptions, or even the shipping fees, don't forget to check the invoices and fee option.

Settings Account

On this page, you'll find all the details required to manage your Shopify account. It essentially provides an account overview, status of the account, and the Shopify plan you opted for. If you have any other staff accounts associated with your main Shopify account, then use the accounts and permissions options to manage all the other accounts. You can pause the store, close your Shopify store, or also hire an expert by using the store status option.

Step 4: Adding Products

Open the dashboard, select products, and then click on the option to add products. In this section, you can add new products to your e-commerce store so that you can sell them immediately. To get started, click on the "add product" button, and provide the required product title and any other additional information associated with the product. There are two methods you can use for uploading products. You can manually add products or bulk import them. To manually add products, you'll need to fill out details for every product like product description, title, image, category, variants, price, and so on. You can also bulk import all the products by importing them via a CSV (comma separated values) file.

If you don't have a product yet, you can use a duplicate product option. Once duplicated, you can make changes as and when you receive the new items. However, if you are interested in adding any variance to a specific product, then don't forget to click on the "add various" button.

Step 5: Assigning Products

Now, it is time to assign different products to various collections. To do this, click on the products option from the navigation menu, then go to collections, and then click on create collections option. Once you have created and added all the products, it is time to segregate them into particular collections. Different collections help to optimize the display of products in the menus available on your e-commerce store.

There are two ways in which you can add products to collections on your Shopify website. The first step is to add the products you want to different collections manually, and the second option is to add products automatically. If you opt for the automated route, then certain products will be automatically added to a specific collection whenever it meets certain preset criteria set by you.

Step 6: Applying Themes

Now, it is time to apply themes to your Shopify store. The first step is to open the dashboard, then visit the online store. Go to option setting and select themes. The Shopify theme store is quite simple to use, and you can get started with it right away. There are various free and paid-for themes available to choose from on Shopify. Every theme on Shopify comes with a preview. So, you can see the preview before you decide to apply it to your store. Once you opt for a specific theme, all you need to do is publish it on the Shopify store. You will learn more about the different themes available in the subsequent chapters.

Step 7: Customization

Customizing the navigation bar is also an important part of creating your Shopify store. The first step is to open the Shopify store, go to the sales channel section, and then click on the online store. In this option, opt for navigation, and from there on, click on the menu to add the links you want to add. In this space, you can add different navigational links a user can use to view your online store. You can add links to the "About Us" page, policy page, or even the "contact us" page. Think about all the different pages you wish to include in the Shopify website and then add the links for these in the navigation bar.

Step 8: Pages

You cannot have a website that doesn't have any pages on it. Once you have added all the links required, you then need to create the respective pages for them as well. To create pages, open the dashboard, and visit the online store option, and click on pages. There are different pages your website must include, such as the "about us," "contact information," FAQs, and policy pages. Ensure that these pages provide all the information a potential customer might need before purchasing from your e-commerce store.

Step 9: Blogs

You can also add blog posts and blog categories such as e-commerce news to your website. By adding some valuable content to the website, you are increasing the value it offers potential customers. When your customers know they stand to gain something from accessing your website, then their inclination to access your website will increase. It is also a great way to retain your customers while increasing loyalty.

Step 10: Customizing Themes

In the previous step, you were asked to select a theme for your Shopify store. After you select a theme, it is time to customize the theme to make your store look more attractive. During customization, you are required to upload the logo for your store, upload any slides of product images or deals to place a carousel feature on your homepage. You can also add related item functionality for all the product pages. In customization, you are required to choose the number of items that will show up on each line of the collection pages. Deciding the product placement and presentation is quite important because it creates the overall feel of the website.

Step 11: Domain

Shopify automatically displays a domain name for your online store. A domain name is the online address of your e-commerce store. Therefore, you need to have a domain name. The domain name should be attractive and easy to understand and remember. Shopify will automatically display a domain name for your e-commerce store free of charge. If you want, you can try this free option or purchase a customized domain name. If the domain name you opt for is already taken, then you are required to change the domain name.

Step 12: Store Preferences

To go through the store preferences, you need to go to the dashboard, click on the online store option, and then go to preferences from there. Ensure that you carefully go through all the different categories present in the store preferences option. The different categories, you need to pay attention to include Google analytics, title and Meta description, password protection, Facebook pixel, and checkout protection. The title and Meta description help ensure that your e-commerce store is optimized for search engines. By adding some Meta content to this, it allows the search engines to crawl and index your store, thereby increasing your online visibility. By enabling Google Analytics, you can keep track of all the visitors who visit the store. It also generates reports about different metrics and data you can use to come up with actionable insights for the sake of better marketing plans. As soon as your store is ready to go live, uncheck the password to make your store globally accessible. If you have or wish to launch a Facebook ad campaign, then enter the Facebook pixel ID to create online advertising campaigns. It helps track conversions, find new customers, and concentrate your marketing efforts. To protect your e-commerce store on Shopify from spam or abuse, complete the Google reCAPTCHA option at checkout.

Step 13: Paying for Shopify

Once you go through all these steps, it is time to select a specific Shopify plan to get started. There are five different plans available on Shopify, and they are as follows.

Shopify Lite

Shopify Lite costs $9 a month. If you are new to Shopify or want a trial run, then this is the cheapest option available. With Shopify Lite, you can showcase products on an existing website to different users on Facebook, and use Shopify to manage the sale of products, even at physical locations. If you have an existing website, then this option will come in handy.

Basic Shopify

Basic Shopify costs $ 29 per month, and it is the cheapest option available if you want to create your own e-commerce store on this platform. The various features it offers are unlimited file storage, supports two user accounts, allows you to sell unlimited products, offers customer support 24 hours a day, seven days a week, provides broad analysis, helps generate discount codes, and also supports the blog. Apart from this, it also supports manual order creation, offers complete access to e-commerce features, and helps recover abandoned carts.

Shopify

This plan from Shopify costs $79 per month, and it offers greater functionality benefits than the previous plans. It helps generate gift cards, recover abandoned carts at a better rate, provide advanced reports, and reduce the transaction fees. It also reduces the credit card fees payable on this platform. The option to generate gift cards will come in handy for any brand that desires to improve its recognition in the market. This plan from Shopify offers detailed summaries of customer and sales reports. It's ideal for anyone who has a high volume of online sales, sells products on gift cards can be issued, and requires detailed reports.

Advanced Shopify

This plan from Shopify costs $299 per month. With this plan, two functionalities are offered in addition to the ones offered by the previous plans. It not only offers advanced reports but also provides information about real-time shipping. This plan allows you to manage all the Shopify data easily while you create easily customizable reports. You can select from a variety of dimensions and metrics to create customized reports and save them for future reference. There are also a variety of filters you can apply to the data to obtain specific results that you wish to view.

Shopify Plus

This plan from Shopify costs $ 2000 per month. While this plan is the most expensive one available on Shopify. It is usually best suited to large companies instead of small and medium enterprises. This is a corporate solution that essentially offers all the features that have been mentioned up until now, and additional advanced functionalities like order fulfillment, security, and an application programming interface. Don't opt to do this unless you have an extremely high volume of sales, require advanced integration between the e-commerce store and other internal software, and have a massive budget.

Go through these different plans and opt for one that suits all your needs and requirements.

Step 14: Installing Apps

When it comes to Shopify, there are several thousands of apps to choose from. All these apps can be easily integrated with your e-commerce store. However, it is important to choose the right apps. The different apps you can use will help promote the online store, reward your customers, take care of shipping, track to revenue you on, and even manage inventory. Every function that you can think of that's necessary to run and maintain an e-commerce store can be taken care of by installing the app. Therefore, ensure that you carefully go through the list of different apps discussed in the subsequent chapters.

You merely need to follow the different steps given in this section to create a Shopify store within no time.

CHAPTER THREE

CHOOSING THE RIGHT SHOPIFY THEME

If you run an online business, you know that viewers will judge your website based on its look and feel. Therefore, you must choose the right theme for your store. In this chapter, we will look at things you must consider when you choose a theme for your store. Remember, the right theme will help your store stand out.

- Why is it important to pick the perfect theme?

- Most store owners tend to ask the following questions:

- Does the theme have to do certain things?

- Does the layout of the store matter?

- Will visitors care about the images and colors used on the website?

Try to understand that the layout and theme of your store will sum up your products and brand. You can visually represent your business by using the right theme. It can also have a significant effect on your store in terms of trustworthiness, conversion rates, and more. The Internet has a lot of information about how your online store should be, which theme layouts you must choose, and why. Research says that most users look for an 'F' shaped pattern on a website. This means the websites that have a strong and effective header and sidebar on the left-hand side of the page are what users will prefer.

Another thing you must note is that good website design and theme is a strong indicator of trust. If the website looks shady, then it will become a little tricky to gain the trust of your target audience. Some businesses are doing it right, and one such business is Speck and Stone. This store sells beautiful products, but what catches the eye of a customer in the store's design. They have designed the website beautifully. The store uses the Brooklyn theme available in the Shopify Theme Store and has customized the theme to fit their brand and business. The website feels and looks right. This is a hard thing to explain, but when you look at their store, you will understand what all this means. A lot of time was spent by the business owners to try and test different themes before they settled with a theme.

The business owners understood what their customers were looking for because they sell a product that is unique and visual. The Brooklyn theme helps them convey this message via large images, simple navigation, and clear call to actions. If you have the perfect theme, you can achieve a storefront like Speck and Stone.

Things to do Before You Pick a Theme

Some people might get overwhelmed when there is plenty of choices available, and they need to select one theme for their store. If you have never built an online store, and this is your first experience, then it will be difficult to understand what your business or brand requires. You should start with the default theme when you set up the store. Shopify allows you to customize this theme and play around with some features. Alternatively, you can start with a new theme as well. There is nothing wrong with sticking to the default theme if you are using Shopify for the first time. This theme works very well, and customers can navigate easily. You can also learn how different features work. You should play around with this theme before you move onto choosing other themes. Here are some questions you should ask yourself when you look at themes:

- What features should I include on the website?

- How do I want the customers to experience my store?

- How can I emulate what my competitors are doing?

- What layout should I use to display the products?

- How many products should I display in the store?

- Have I set aside a budget for a theme? Or should I select a free theme?

Don't ever make your choice based on fonts and colors. You can always change these features later. You can only move forward when you answer the above questions. You can start nailing some criteria for your theme. This will point you in the right direction. Once you consider the questions above, you can head to the Theme Store and look at the different themes available. You can also work with a Shopify expert if you want something unique. If you have enough startup or working capital, you can work with a designer to set up your store.

Enter the Theme Store

The Shopify Theme Store has over 100 different themes that you can use for your store. The in-house design team develops most themes, while third-party developers develop some. Experts recommend that you use themes from the Shopify theme store. The marketing team evaluates every theme submitted by designers for functionality and quality before it lists them in the store.

Improved Search Tools

You can use different filters in the Shopify theme store to search for the right theme.

A filter will allow you to browse different themes based on the industry, layout, purpose, and features. You can use the following filter:

- Layout Style

- Inventory Size

- Social Features

- Product Type

- Home Page Features and more

You must narrow down the options, so you can focus on the features that you want to use, depending on the experience you want to create for your customers. You can use the search option to look for key terms, specific features, and theme designers. You can use different collections to browse themes. The Shopify team curates and develops these collections and updates them based on new releases, style, features, and trending themes. You can look at other stores as an example and get inspiration from their stores. This will also help you determine the customization possibilities within this theme.

If you want to see how the theme would look for your store, you can use the demo stores option. You must understand that this option only shows you what you can do if you use the theme. You can always customize the theme with your photography, content, and branding. You can also read theme reviews to understand how other storeowners liked the theme. When you find a theme that has some or all the features you need, you should check the App Store to see how you can extend the functionality of the theme.

Base Your Decision on Theme Support

You must consider theme support when you choose the perfect theme for your store. If you choose a free theme, you can get support from the Theme Support Team. You can always reach out to them if you have any questions about the functionality and features of the theme. If a third-party developer designs a theme, you can reach out to their support team for help. If you do use a third-party design, you must directly speak to their support team if you have any questions or issues. Since Shopify works with vetted developers, you can trust them to answer all your questions and queries about themes. These developers know the theme inside out and can answer any questions you have about the theme.

Test and Experiment

You now know that you have different options to choose from. You also know how you should pick the theme. But how do you pick the perfect theme for your store? You should take your time to test a theme and experiment with its layout, functionality, and features. You can work with different free themes and see how they work for you. Compare how these will work for your brand before you choose the theme that is best for you. There is no better way to find the right theme for your store than to use the questions, sorting features, and criteria mentioned above.

Tips to Choose a Shopify Themes

Apart from the tips mentioned above, you can consider the following points when you pick out the Shopify Theme.

Understand the Limitations

Shopify is a great platform with tons of features and benefits. This platform does have its limitations. Many users either do not know about these limitations or choose to overlook them. Remember, no Shopify theme will give you a complete website. People tend to enter the Shopify Theme Store and believe they will find the theme that has everything they need. This is normally not the case.

When you look for a theme, you should look for one that will cover 80% of what you are looking for. You can deal with the remaining 20% during the next phase. If it is urgent, you can hire a designer who can complete this for you. Shopify does not allow you to customize every page the way you want to. Every Shopify theme has sections. These sections are drag and drop elements that you can play around with to design the store. It is simple to use these elements, but these elements will limit the functionality and capability of that section. You cannot drag and drop a product or image wherever you want.

When you select a theme on Shopify, you can work with various sections. You can add slideshows, videos, or images to these sections and move them around. You can also open each section to see what content you want to add. Shopify also allows you to organize the content. You must understand that Shopify will allow you to use sections only on the home, collection, and product pages. This means you cannot use the same sections across all other pages in your store. Every other page on your store will have the same static builder. You can always add text, images, and videos, but not the same way if you were using sections. Some themes allow you to add some sections to pages that are not the home collection or product pages. This will require some additional work.

Stick to the Shopify Theme Store

Since you are aware of the limitations of the store, you need to spend some time and look at the different themes. Experts recommend that you select a theme within the Shopify store. As mentioned earlier, Shopify will evaluate the themes sent to the store for functionality and quality before it lists them on the website. They also ensure that these themes abide by the latest policies of Shopify. Therefore, when you choose a theme from the Shopify store, you know it complies with all rules and regulations.

When you select a theme from the Shopify Theme Store, you will get great support. Every theme has its own support, and you can reach out if you have any questions or issues. You can also speak to the support team if you have any general queries as well. Not every theme developer provides this support. Therefore, before you choose the theme, you should speak to the support team and see how they respond to you. You can find the name of the theme developer on the bottom left corner of the page. Some examples of theme developers that offer great support are Pixel Union, Groupthought, Archetype Themes, and Out of the Sandbox. Experts suggest that you should not choose free themes since they lack functionality and support that paid themes have. You can use free themes if you want to test and experiment with them, but you should avoid using them to build the store or brand. Remember, you always get what you pay for, and when you use a paid theme, you will get a lot more.

Do not Choose Themes Because They Match Your Products

When you filter on themes based on the industry or product type, you will come across different mock themes that sell the products you are selling. Remember, this does not make these themes a great fit for your store. This might be the case in some situations, but it does not always work. The theme that you believe suits your product or store may not have the functionality or features you are looking for. For example, if you are looking to filter themes based on the industry, the themes in the store are only suggestions. You do not have to stick to these themes. You can use the theme for the Fashion industry as well if it suits your purpose.

When you look at theme previews, do not focus only on the products that the theme demo is selling. You should focus on the type of content, the ease of navigation, the layout, sections, etc. For example, some themes need large product images to look good. Do not make the mistake of choosing a website only because it has the images of the products you are selling. If you selected a theme with large images, but you only have small images of your product, the layout will not work for you.

Identify the Features You Want to Include

Before you go through different themes, understand the features you want to include on your page. If you are unsure of the features you should include, you can go through different themes and look at the features on each theme. Once you do this, you can make a list of the main features of these themes. When you have this list, you can look for a theme that has a majority of these features and fits well with your brand. Remember, you want to select a theme that has most of the features you are looking for. This way, you can cut down on development costs. This means if you find a theme that has two amazing features but ten features you do not want to use, do not select that theme. You should always choose a theme that has more of the features you want. You can speak to the developer and ask him to add any missing features to it. The theme preview page lists the main features of the theme. Most times, this list is not exhaustive. It is for this reason that you must look at the demo of the theme and play around with it before you select the theme. The best way to do this is to create a development store from a Shopify partner's account. When you have this account, you can create a development store and play around with any theme on Shopify for free. You can view all the sections and most features, but you cannot change the code.

Use a Mobile-Friendly Theme

A common mistake plenty of eCommerce storeowners make is they don't pay attention to how their page would look on a mobile phone. The desktop view theme is of utmost importance, but you must understand that most traffic comes from a mobile phone. People are always browsing through different products during their commute. Therefore, you must select a theme that is compatible with a mobile phone. The layout should be easy for the user to navigate or make purchases.

You must optimize any theme you choose to increase conversions. You may believe that every store on Shopify is optimized for conversions. What you must understand is that some stores do better than others because they know how customers think. Most themes do not have the best practices to optimize conversions, but some are better than others, so you must keep an eye out for them. For instance, you must ensure that your customers can add products to the cart. This does sound very simple, but some themes are better than others.

When you look at products from the desktop, you can see the entire product image, price, product name, variants, and the button to add the product to the cart. You do not have to scroll to look for these options. You must ensure that you have the same layout on your mobile phone. When you view a product, you should add the cart button on the page, so a customer does not have to scroll to add the product to the cart. This means customers can easily add products to their cart.

CHAPTER FOUR

DESIGNING YOUR SITE

The design of your Shopify e-commerce store can either attract or repel your customers quite quickly. So, one step you cannot overlook is the e-commerce store design. You don't need to invest all your hard-earned money on designers or any fancy graphics. Some of the best performing stores on Shopify feature intuitive design, simple layout, and plenty of organization. There are three simple rules you must always keep in mind while designing your Shopify store, and they are as follows.

- The overall organization of the store must be your priority.

- The store must be easy to navigate, and the layout needs to be intuitive.

- The store design needs to be attractive and not distracting.

In this chapter, we'll go through each of these elements and simple tips you can use to optimize your store design on Shopify.

The Homepage

The homepage of your e-commerce store is equivalent to the display window of a regular brick and mortar store. The homepage must showcase your lead items, the best products your business has to offer, and any other promotional offers available on the website. Let us look at the different features of the homepage that you need to pay attention to. While designing the e-commerce store on Shopify.

The Shipping Bar

Regardless of whether you offer free shipping or not, always include a shipping bar on your e-commerce store is quintessential. You can also use the space provided for the shipping bar to advertise any coupon codes, promotions, or any other advertising tactic to increase conversions. The shipping bar must be enabled on every page of the e-commerce store to remind customers about your shipping policies or any promotions while they go about browsing through the different products on your website. You also have an option to install a responsive shipping bar while using Shopify.

So, what is a responsive shipping bar? The responsive shipping bar automatically starts counting down the price of potential customers who need to add to their cart to avail of free shipping. For instance, let us assume that the free shipping threshold for your website is $ 35, and a visitor has added an item worth $29 to his cart. If you enable a responsive shipping bar, then it will start counting backward to show the visitor that he merely needs to add another $6 worth of items to a whale free shipping.

Navigation Menu

The logo and navigation menu needs to be placed directly below the shipping bar. Try to place them in the same row so that the header doesn't take up much space on the homepage. Also, the header must not take up more than 15% of the page space available above the fold. Above the fold refers to the area on the screen that is visible to the viewer without scrolling down. Keep in mind that the most important elements present on the screen should always be above the fold, especially on the checkout and product pages.

The logo for your e-commerce website needs to be attractive and simple. It should be small enough so that it easily fits within the confines of the header bar and should be clear so that the viewer knows it is associated with your brand. Always place the navigation menu horizontally in the header section of the page. The different sections to be included in the navigation menu are the homepage, catalog, about us, contact us, and another page for tracking and shipment. The tracking page is optional, but all the other elements must always be included in the navigation menu and your e-commerce website. You are free to add as many pages as you want, but ensure that the navigation menu doesn't exceed five items at any given time. More than five items, and it will make the page look quite cluttered and crowded.

Try to position the catalog towards the front of the list. Most people usually read from left to right, so the pages need to be arranged so that the most important sections are always displayed first. Also, if you have more than ten products, the product catalog should be organized into a collection list, which drops down from the navigation menu. A well-structured catalog not only lends organization to the overall web page but also gives customers the help required to find the products that they are looking for quickly.

This brings us to the next important page in the navigation menu, and that is the contact us page. Ensure that it is easy to access this page since it can be critical when it comes to making sales. At times, various issues may arise associated with product defects, order cancellations, or even shipping. If your customers or potential customers cannot reach you or they don't know where to reach you, the chances are that they will not purchase anything from your website. Also, a website without a legitimate Contact Us page looks dubious. The contact us page must always include information about support, email address, hours of operation, phone numbers, and also support form.

Banner Image

The banner image is also known as the hero shot and is often placed below the navigation menu. In this place, you can post any promotional information about new products, product launches, or any current offers or sales. All your branding efforts are further amplified when you place a banner image, and it also lends a sense of attractiveness to your homepage. Don't merely place a banner image, because there's supposed to be one on the page. Ensure that you use this section wisely to increase your overall sales. So, avoid using a random stock photo, which holds little or no significance for the business website. The banner image should be well thought out and is an incredibly important part of the home page. You can use the banner image to call attention to the latest products, featured collection, or even to place a compelling call to action to increase your sales.

Featured Collection

Every business has its best-selling or lead items. So, it is time to ensure that the homepage of your e-commerce business also contains some space dedicated exclusively to showcasing your best-selling items, or multiple collections. Start by making a list of the newest and most popular items you have in store. Once you have this list, it is time to integrate them into your homepage to capture the viewer's attention and encourage them to shop. However, while doing this, ensure that you are not merely dumping images of various products onto the homepage.

Product dumping is quite chaotic, and it merely refers to dumping multiple rows of unrelated products on the homepage, hoping that someone will find it attractive. Well, no one is going to take this clumsy bait, and all it does is make your e-commerce store look unattractive. Your e-commerce store will look disorganized, sloppy, and the customers will be visually put off. Also, the featured collection needs to be small and should ideally fit within a single row of products. While creating the featured collection, ensure that the products you choose are quite similar in nature.

If you are interested in adding more than five products to the featured collection, ensure that it is set in a carousel format. By using a carousel format, your viewers can seamlessly and effortlessly scroll through all the different products presented in a collection that catches their interest.

The Footer

The footer of the website includes the newsletter, logo, legal pages, links to any of your other social media accounts, hours of operation, and links for customer support. You can also use this to include trust seals and trust badges or any other guarantees your website provides. Ensure that all the sales badges you decide to use are in sync with your store's overall policies.

Social Proof

Social proof is based on a simple concept that people tend to follow instinctive actions. If you include a little social proof on your homepage, you can easily lend some uniqueness and authenticity to your brand. It can also make your website seem more attractive to any of the potential visitors. The various forms of social proof you can include are a link to your Instagram or any other social media profile, any blogs, or even testimonials. You don't have to limit yourself to one type of social proof and can include a variety of all these three things on the homepage. You can use an application such as the Loox to seamlessly integrate any product reviews into your homepage to act as social proof.

Exit-Intent Pop-Up

The exit intent pop-up isn't something that doesn't necessarily show up on the homepage. As its name suggests, it usually pops up as soon as a visitor is about to leave a site. As an e-commerce store owner, your primary aim must be to create a seamless experience that appeals to your visitors. So, while your potential customers are shopping or going through the website, don't harangue them by constantly interrupting their shopping experience so that they can subscribe to a newsletter for a storefront they aren't fully familiar with. If you do this, your chances to increase leads will reduce. Ensure that the color scheme it follows is the same as the e-commerce store matches the pop-up's design.

A simple exit intent pop-up could be something like, "Wait! By entering your email address, you can take advantage of a 10% discount," or "Hello the first-time shopper! Enter your email address to get a 10% instant discount." The simple idea to incentivize data collection for your customers makes it easier to obtain their email address. Keep in mind that the incentive needs to be attractive and should compel the visitor to provide his email address. When you create the exit intent pop-up, ensure that you limit the number of fields present in the form and restrict it to only the visitor's email address.

The Catalog

There are a couple of important features you need to consider product images and layout when it comes to in between pages. Always try to design the product catalog page so that it can easily fit at least 25 images per page, so all the products will essentially be displayed in the form of five products for five rows. The primary aim of your store's overall design should be to offer simple navigation for the user. Therefore, it means you must try to reduce the time the user spends when he has to scroll or sift through the different pages on the website. All the product images you use must be uniform in size, as well as having a uniform composition. The product images must not only be of the same size but must be shot from the same angle and have the same backdrop. When there is consistency in all this, your e-commerce store will look more organized, and the product images will look professional. Also, it creates a visual that is easy on the eyes and attractive.

Product Page

The product pages are quite important in the website of any e-commerce store. The product pages not only display all that your store wishes to sell, but they also help convince the visitors to make a purchase. Here is a simple tip about product images that you can keep in mind while you create the product pages-though product image, which loads on the product page, which must be the same as the one you used in the catalog. Ensure that the page isn't redirected to an image of a product from a different angle. Also, line up the images so that they are congruent when you move from one page to another.

After the Fold

Certain features need to be easily accessible, and your customers shouldn't have to search for these features. They need to be readily accessible and noticeable. Usually, the elements are placed toward the right side of the page, and they include product price, title, any available variants, and the add cart button. The left side of the product page should ideally display the product image and all the other thumbnails. Ensure that the product thumbnails always lie below or toward the left of the primary image. To make the product page look clean and organized, set the thumbnails to a carousel function.

Tabbed Product Descriptions

All the information available on your website about product descriptions is presented in bite-sized and easily consumable pieces of information. The visitors merely need to look at these small pieces of information to obtain all the details they require before they make a purchase and don't have to read through blocks of text. The tabs to be included in this aspect include product description, a size chart whenever applicable, shipping and delivery information, directions to use the product, and the reasons why the visitor should choose the product. Ensure that the product description also includes the shipping time estimate.

Add to Cart

The only action button present on the product page must be the add-to-cart button. So, don't include any wish list or social media sharing buttons on the product pages. Also, ensure that the add-to-cart button is quite different from all the other buttons present on the different pages, and other elements.

Product Reviews

The ideal place to display the product review section will be right at the footer of the product page. Every product you display on the website needs to have its own product review section. Are you wondering why reviews are important? Well, if you have ever shopped online, it is quite likely that you would have scrolled through various reviews to determine whether the product lives up to its expectations or not. Or maybe you would look at the reviews to gauge the worthiness of the seller. Likewise, anyone who's shopping on your website will also want to know the genuine nature and authenticity of the product or services you are supplying. Include some strong and positive customer reviews to earn your audience's trust in your business.

Recommended Products

A simple tactic for plenty of e-commerce stores and businesses to increase the average cart value is to show a list of recommended products. For each section of the product page, ensure that you include a recommended products section. All the recommendations need to be complementary or related to the main products played on the page, or else this technique will prove to be redundant. The recommended products must be created such that they help target the visitor's interest. So, it doesn't make any sense to link any irrelevant products because it will not increase the average cart value. Did you ever shop on Amazon? Whenever you view a specific product, the product page displays a list of recommended products based on the product you viewed. It is a simple tactic used to encourage the visitor to increase the cart value. For instance, if your Shopify store sells surfboards, then recommended products can be leashes, wax, wetsuits, or even surf racks. An obvious point you should keep in mind while creating the list of recommended products is that the product offering must be included in your product catalog.

Sticky Add to Cart Button

Regardless of whether you are on the homepage or the product page, you can quickly add a specific product to the cart, if you use sticky add to cart buttons on the website. Perhaps the visitor sees something in the product description that compelled him to buy. Instead of clicking on the specific product page and then adding it to the cart, the visitor can quickly add it to his cart from any page and then proceed to checkout. The sticky cart helps eliminate any unnecessary scrolling and allows the visitor to take the required action and move toward purchase immediately.

Overall Theme

Up until now, we have covered all the important aspects to design the perfect Shopify store for your e-commerce business. The last aspect you must concentrate on is the theme. The theme essentially brings everything together and adds a sense of cohesiveness to your website. Shopify offers a variety of free and paid-for themes. Select the theme that works well with your product or service offering and the kind of business feel you wish to create.

You will learn more about the different types of themes to choose from in the next chapter. Carefully go through all the different design elements discussed in this chapter and make the required changes to your Shopify store.

CHAPTER FIVE

SHOPIFY APPLICATIONS

Shopify not only makes it easier for you to sell online, but it also provides every online store what it needs to succeed. Some Shopify applications are valuable resources to use if you want to boost your sales. Every Shopify store owner wants to do this. It is a bit overwhelming to navigate through the app store and test over 2,000 applications to find the right one for you. This chapter will list the best applications you can use for your store. These are the best ways to increase your conversions and leads at a low cost.

Boost Sales

This is the only application that offers both cross-selling and upselling. It is believed that close to 35% of Amazon's revenue comes from cross-selling and upselling. This strategy is one of the best ways to increase your revenue only when you know how to use it. Boost Sales is one of the best applications to help you do this. This is not the only application in the Shopify App Store that enables upselling and cross-selling, but it stands out from the other applications for many reasons such as:

- Customization

- Professional design

- Reporting capabilities

When a customer views an item or adds it to the cart, this application will recommend other related products to the customer. This way, you can bring more value to the customers and retain them. You can also bring in more sales using this application. The application also allows you to create an upsell or cross-sell offer in a pop-up or widget form.

KIT

This application offers an extra set of hands that will help you with marketing or advertising your store. KIT is your free virtual employee, and it will automatically recommend various marketing activities you can use to drive sales. You can create discount codes and promote that code over Facebook Messenger or SMS using KIT. You can also do the following:

- Thank customers via emails or messages

- Retarget customers to bring them back to your store

- Convert visitors into potential customers and more.

- KIT also helps you grow your business by managing the following:

- Facebook advertisement

- Instagram advertisements

- Social posts

- Email marketing

It does all this for free. When you use KIT, you can increase your sales. You can let the application take care of your marketing.

Checkout Boost

Regardless of whether you run a small or a big store, you may be unknowingly bleeding money. It usually happens because of the following reasons.

- Visitors or leads you could not convert as customers

- Abandoned carts

- Customers who left the website before they completed the payment

- Sales that you could not upsell and more

The Checkout Boost app is the best way to solve this problem. This application will allow you to create different deals to increase the checkouts by up to 25%. You can use this application to run an exit-intent offer to catch any visitor or customer who may do not complete their purchase. You can use the Sales Gamification technique to offer users special discounts to motivate them to purchase the product. The application also allows you to upsell relevant items after the customer has checked out the products. You can offer customers special discounts or offers if they share their cart on social media. You can make a lot of money when you use the Checkout Boost application.

Countdown Cart

When people believe a specific product is low in supply, they will buy more of it. As a business owner, you must understand human psychology. You can make a lot of money if you know how to create scarcity and a strong sense of urgency with this simple psychological tactic. If you do not know how you can achieve this, use Countdown Cart. This application will add a countdown timer on your page and will count the stock. You can also add a widget that will share the count on social media pages. When you do this, you can nudge your customers and shoppers to complete their purchases. This application will increase the chances of conversion.

Moosend

You can also use email marketing to target visitors. Moosend is a platform that allows you to automate the process of email marketing. This application lets you track any visitor's behavior and customer's purchase behavior. It will then find a pattern and recommend specific products to the visitor or customer. You should use every piece of data you have collected to leverage your mailing list. You can create a workflow and trigger it to send an email to every customer or visitor on your mailing list. This workflow will store customer purchase history. If the customer abandons the cart, this application will send a follow-up email. This will restore your revenue. You can also define a sequence to greet your customers. You can use Moosend to connect with 1000 subscribers every month. You can send unlimited emails to those subscribers for free. When you upgrade, you can access more features to help you generate leads.

SiteKit

You can use this application to create different pop-ups for your store. You can include coupon pop-ups, top bars, even spin-to-win pop-ups, and free shipping bars. The application is a great way to promote your sales and campaigns. You can also build a mailing list with the email IDs of all customers. You can use coupon codes to incentivize customers to purchase products. You can also ask them to subscribe to any marketing emails.

Sales Pop

Sales Pop is one of the most popular applications, and you must know how to use it. This application was launched in 2017 and is one of the most popular applications used in Shopify. It has over 8,000 reviews and 60,000 active users. This application moved to the best sales application in just a week. This application creates credibility. It will show customers what products other customers purchased and from where. This motivates customers to purchase products and boosts the conversion rate for your page. Once you install this application, it will retrieve the latest orders from your data and turn those into notification pop-ups.

Personalized Recommendation

This application analyzes every user's sales history and browser behavior to identify the user's unique preferences. This application will use this information to display product recommendations relevant to the customer across the website to create a better shopping experience for the customers.

You can build five widgets on your page using this application. These widgets will give you the option to set the appropriate type of recommendation.

- Customers who purchased this product also purchased _____

- The best products in the store

- Featured recommendations and recently viewed

Recommendations using a Smart upsell pop-up to increase the number of products added to the cart. This will help you boost sales. When a customer adds these items to the cart using the recommendation widget, the application will pop up a clean upsell that will suggest other items related to this product.

If you are interested in cross-selling and upselling, you can also use the Boost Sales. We have covered this application earlier in this chapter.

Smile.io

Smile.io will always allow you to set up a rewards program quickly. You can use this program to motivate your customers and engage them, regardless of whether they are on your website on both a desktop and mobile phone. When you reward a customer, he will be more loyal and will likely return to the website to become a repeat purchaser. You can also create reward programs for customer referrals, purchases, social shares, or follows, birthday rewards, and account registrations in a few clicks.

Snapppt

The developers designed this application to link your Instagram account to the Shopify store. This will help you increase sales for your business. Snapppt helps to bridge the gap between your store and your Instagram account. Your profile page on Snapppt will display all the images you post on Instagram. It will also allow customers to move to that part of the store where they can find the product directly. This application will allow you to add images from Instagram to your Snapppt profile and embed a link to these images, so it leads customers to the right page when they select the image.

Snapppt also allows you to embed your profile into any part or page of your website or store. This will create a seamless experience. When you use Snapppt, you can make Instagram one of the easiest ways to acquire customers. You can also motivate followers to purchase the products they see on your Instagram profile.

Auto Currency Switcher

If your business is spread globally, ensure that all the visitors and customers can view the products in the currency used in their country. When customers can see the prices in their home currency, they don't have to calculate the conversion rates. You can also allow your customers to change the currency using the dropdown near the currency. The checkout must still remain in the shop's currency. This application will increase the comfort of a foreign customer and increase your sales across the globe.

Facebook Shop

When you use this application, you can sell products on your store directly on Facebook. When you activate the sales channel on Facebook with Shopify, it will allow you to add a Shop tab on Facebook where it will display the Shopify products. Customers can check out quickly while on Facebook, either through their mobile or desktop. You can also manage inventory, order, and product with Shopify. This application will allow you to grow your reach.

Happy Email

This application is not only a full email marketing solution but is simple to use too. It also allows you to send customers welcome emails when they sign up. You can also send emails to your customers to thank them for their purchase on your e-commerce store. The best thing about this application is that it sends emails from the founder's account immediately after the purchase. You can use this application to uplift the engagement between your store and the customers by establishing a personal connection.

Bulk Image Edit

Remember to optimize images used in the store. This is an essential part of any online business. This application will allow you to optimize the size of images and set meaningful and apt Alt Text for each product. You can also optimize the images used in the theme. When you use Bulk Image Edit, you can increase the traffic to your website. If you have the right format and images, you can convert leads into customers, thereby generating sales.

Best Coupon Box

You can use this application to increase your sales and add more customers or leads to your email list. Better Coupon Box will help you offer customers special discounts. You can also suggest discounts to new subscribers or followers. This incentive will encourage visitors to buy the product, thereby converting the visitor into a customer. You can also collect email IDs from these users and build a larger mailing list. You can use this email list to target the right customers. Your customers will trust you more when you give them greater value. They will also sign up to your social pages and refer your products to other customers.

Gorgias

This is one of the leading customer service applications and is exclusively for Shopify stores. You can improve customer service by using this application. Using the

Gorgias Shopify helpdesk, you can centralize customer service and communication across all channels, right from live chat to emails and even Facebook comments. This will help you build visibility across all channels. You can use this to leverage your sales promotions and campaigns. When you integrate this application with Shopify, you can perform key actions on orders and customer profiles. This application will help you save time.

Custom Options

Shopify only allows you to perform three customizations on your product page. If you want to make other customizations, you should use this application. Using this application, you can add unlimited customizations and personalize different products. This will help you give your customers what they want, thereby increasing your sales. This application allows you to create an unlimited list of products your customers can choose from.

Spocket

Regardless of whether you want to add products to your store or start a new store, you should consider Spocket. This application will help you source products from the US and Europe and offers you a marketplace for Shopify drop-shipping. You can access this marketplace for free. The team vets the suppliers in the marketplace regularly.

These suppliers also offer discounts to your customers. You can embed Spocket to your Shopify store. Once you do this, you can find products and list them on your product page.

Easyship

This application will help you sell products internationally. An Easyship account will give you access to over 100 worldwide carriers. Easyship also offer discounts of up to 70% and provides information on the following:

- Taxes and duties

- Shipping regulations

- Couriers and tariffs

All you need to do is connect your store to this application, download the orders and print the labels and other paperwork. This application is free, but you must bear the shipping costs.

Regardless of whether you have a store that is big or small, you can take advantage of these applications. Remember to use these applications appropriately since that will help to increase your sales. If you can spend close to $0 and improve sales, why not invest in one of these applications?

CHAPTER SIX

SETTING UP THE EMAIL LIST

You don't necessarily have to place excessive emphasis on your Shopify store's overall rate of conversion. However, it is important to spend a little time on first-time visitors, especially from any low intent channels (the ones who require the most convincing to ensure that they make a purchase), is a good idea. How do you think this can be done? Well, this is where email marketing steps in. In this world of social media, email marketing might sound a little old-fashioned. Never underestimate the power of simple email marketing. It is always easier to convince someone to provide their email address on the first visit to your store than talk them into a purchase. Well, it doesn't cost them anything to disclose their email address. When you offer them some value in return, the chances of receiving their email addresses increases.

Regardless of the marketing campaign you wish to launch, it all starts with an email list. The best way to get started is by building a well-targeted and segmented

69

email list. If your list is not properly organized, then there is no point in spending a lot of time and effort to curate special offers and come up with an engaging copy. The three important aspects of creating a good email list are relevancy, quality, and quantity.

Five Ways to Build an Email List

As with the email list you wish to build, your e-commerce store's website is also something that is completely under your control. Keep in mind that some of your most valuable subscribers are shoppers who are interested in what your website offers but did not make a purchase on their first visit. Therefore, it will do you and your business some good to concentrate on the online store as the starting point for building an email list.

Adding a Pop-Up

The one place where pop-ups will come in handy is when the customer is heading towards the back button. Adding an exit-intent pop-up to your e-commerce store is the first opportunity you have to save a potential sale. It is where email pop-ups tend to help. When you make the right offer to the right audience, a pop-up can dramatically increase the number of email sign-ups you receive from the website. To get started, try integrating an exit intent pop-up to your e-commerce store. These pop-ups appear on the website or the webpage only when the user moves the mouse somewhere off the page. It is usually a measure of intention that the user is going to navigate somewhere else and not proceed to the payment part or complete the purchase. You can concentrate on coming up with an email copy that appeals to new customers only.

One type of loss that is hard to recover from is the one where your store loses a visitor before the completion of the sale. So, come up with a couple of simple discounts you can offer to keep the long-term interests of your business in mind. At times, all it takes is a simple discount to convince a user to become a paying loyal customer.

Pop-Up Events

A simple yet effective way in which you can build awareness for your emerging brands is to host a temporary pop-up or pop-in shop. It allows you to obtain product feedback and encourages potential customers to get hands-on experience with the products you have to offer. Also, it is a great opportunity for you to build your email list.

Your efforts to build the email list have to be restricted to the online world necessarily and can easily be obtained from the real world too. All you need to do is keep a clipboard handy and ask all visitors to write down their email addresses and names. Or even better, you can sync up a tablet or a smartphone with your chosen email-marketing tool and ask the visitors to feed all their details into the device directly. You can also encourage potential customers to register or sign up with your business by offering attractive discounts. For instance, an attractive offer could be something like, "Get a 25% discount by signing up for our email list," or "Get $20 discount immediately by signing up for the email list." The sky's the limit when it comes to being creative with the different offers that you can offer your potential customers.

Sign-Up Button for Social Media

There are several reasons why people tend to follow various brands of social media. One most common reason is that they want to stay updated about any new products, offers, or new launches made by a brand. Since you wish to build your brand and increase your email list, start to concentrate your efforts on your social media channels. Keep in mind that not all platforms are necessarily friendly to enter different links or URLs. However, there are various apps and online tools you can use to insert links or CTA buttons on your social media profiles. For instance, you can use all tools such as the LinkTree to add multiple URLs or links to your profile on Instagram. It essentially allows you to set one link that directs all visitors towards a sign-up form. You can also include a call to action button on your e-commerce store's Facebook business page.

Email Sign-Up Forms

In the navigation bar or the website footer, try to include an email sign-up form. Ensure that the placement of these email sign-ups form the strategy and are located in such spots where you know most of the shoppers will look for additional information about the business. Don't expect extremely high conversion rates initially, but over a period, it all adds up and helps build your email list. For instance, if a potential customer starts to make his way down the website's footer to understand more about the business, you can attach that to catch his attention and encourage him to subscribe. It could say something like, "To learn more about (store name) subscribe to our email list," or "Be the first to learn about all the offers by subscribing to our email list!"

Accelerate the Growth of your Email List

Now that you can add new subscribers to the email list, it is time to move on and further increase your list. Here are various tactics you can use to accelerate the growth of your email list.

Using a Chatbot

It has become quite common to use chatbots these days, but not a lot of people truly understand the full potential. It has to offer. It is a simple automation tool that can be easily incorporated into your website using a channel that focuses on messages. Also, it helps save some of your time and effort, which you will have spent to offer good customer service. For instance, Uber offers customer support via a chatbot. Before it directs you to a customer support executive, you need to tick off the reasons why you need support from the list of reasons. If your reasons already exist in the list, then the issue is automatically resolved by the bot without further escalation. You can use a third-party app such as the MobileMonkey by creating targeted marketing campaigns using a custom chatbot. You can also share and offer a special discount using the chatbot campaign to encourage other users to easily submit their email addresses in exchange for the discount.

Don't Ignore Third-Party Tools

There are plenty of apps and online tools available these days that you can use to build and develop your email list. The great news is that some of these apps can easily be incorporated and integrated into your Shopify store. The two of the most popular apps used to do this are Personizely and Spin to Win. Spin to Win is an interesting app that you can use to collect email addresses from your website. As the name suggests, it looks like a Wheel of Fortune that's placed on the homepage with each rung featuring an attractive offer. To increase your email list, try to attract more shoppers to give out their email at risk by getting a chance to spin the wheel.

Running Ads

Ending pages are usually designed, keeping one outcome or a conversion point in mind. Therefore, they are incredibly useful when it comes to building an email list for the business. You can run ads to drive traffic to a specific landing page; you have a unique opportunity to create a page that is free from all distractions. Also, it allows you to measure the results of such an ad campaign easily. So, landing pages are a great place to direct all website traffic. For instance, creating a targeted ad on Facebook and Instagram to drive people to a free audiobook or a downloadable paper that is directly associated with the products of your e-commerce store. For instance, if your Shopify store deals with organic and homemade sauces, you can offer a downloadable guide in the form of a recipe book. By running, ads that directly send your ideal audience to a specific landing page can help you easily obtain their email address. The mere fact that the user clicked on the link itself shows his interest in your business. On the landing page, include some free content the user can download after providing the email address.

Use a Questionnaire

Another simple tactic you can use to engage and interact with your audience is by using a questionnaire. There are various surveys that you can create by using platforms such as Typeform or Google Forms. You can use questionnaires to conduct market research or even crowdsourcing valuable content for the blog on your website. Don't forget to include a form to obtain email addresses. To do this, you can add a note that informs people they will be automatically added to the list upon filling the form or place a question at the end asking them if they would be interested in subscribing to your email list. You can send out these forms to your friends and family members, post it on your Facebook page, and other social media profiles. Don't forget to include a special offer that makes answering the questionnaire seem tempting for your intended audience. For instance, you can include a simple offer, such as, "You will get a special code to get a 10% instant discount upon completion of this questionnaire." To gather more information from your target audience, it would be a good idea to send out the questionnaire before you can launch the website online. So, by the time your business is up and running, you will already have an established base of subscribers.

Quid Pro Quo

The Latin phrase quid pro quo essentially means something in return for something. So, why don't you offer your target audience something that will appeal to them in exchange for their email addresses? However, keep in mind that the readers will not necessarily obtain any value until your first broadcast. So, offer a couple of freebies to tempt them towards divulging their email addresses. Who doesn't like freebies? An immediate reward is an instant motivating factor. Providing a couple of offers, or even downloadable content are some approaches you can use to obtain email addresses. You can also work on exploring partnerships with other complementary brands to come up with an offer. For instance, if your Shopify store deals with homemade and organic sources, you can offer a discount coupon to another store that sells cooking utensils. This way, you not only gain a partner for marketing, but it also helps your overall online visibility.

If you are unsure of how much an average subscriber is genuinely worth to your Shopify business, think about offers that only have an upfront cost without any ongoing costs once the offer is completed. The simplest technique is by offering a free guide in the form of any additional tips or tricks associated with the product category of business deals. In such situations, the only upfront costs incurred are the time you spend toward creating the content or effort toward designing it. Offering something of value, regardless of whether it is a physical product or information, will always work in your favor.

Holding Contests

You can quickly accelerate the growth of your email list by holding contests and giveaways on social media. It also helps in building brand awareness. Though additional momentum provided by a contest is incredibly valuable during the early days of a business. When your subscriber list is still small, and you don't have much traffic, leverage the power of social media to hold contests, and create awareness. The simplest way to multiply this strategy is, we're partnering with other e-commerce brands that sell products that perfectly complement the ones listed on your website. When you choose the right partner, it becomes easier to make the offer more compelling.

Another simple option you can use is to reach out to influencers who are doing well in your niche. Spend some time, go through different social media profiles, and look for influencers in your chosen niche. Once you identify them, it is time to reach out to them. You can easily partner with them by offering a small fee, product samples, or anything else, depending on the negotiations. Partnering with influencers is a great way to open up your brand to a vast audience base. Instead of waiting to build a following, you can leverage the power of the influencer's existing fan base.

Keep in mind that email marketing is more of an art and not an exact science. So, don't be disheartened if all the tips don't work well for your business. However, each tip can be easily customized to meet the needs of your business. Experiment with all the tips until you find the right ones.

SHOPIFY

CHAPTER SEVEN

MARKETING YOUR SHOPIFY STORE

The idea of any Shopify store is to increase the traffic, and overall rate of conversions. Even if you know the goal you are going after, it can become a little tricky to choose the ideal marketing tactics to attain the goals. As an e-commerce store, you cannot increase your sales unless the traffic on your website is high. It is not just the traffic that matters, but the rate of conversion matters too. In this section, let us look at some effective marketing tactics you can use to market your Shopify store online effectively. Don't be in a rush, and don't try to implement all the ideas at once. Instead, pace yourself and try implementing them one at a time. By doing this, you can effectively figure out the strategies that are and aren't effective for your business.

Before we get started with learning about marketing the Shopify store, it is important to understand what e-commerce marketing means. E-commerce marketing is a simple practice of using various promotional methods to drive traffic to a specific online store, converting the said traffic into paying customers, and retaining the customers while increasing the customer base. An ideal e-commerce strategy consists of various marketing tactics that help build brand awareness, improve customer loyalty and customer retention, and ultimately lead to an increase in the overall sales of a business. You can use the tactics discussed in this section to promote your online store or increase the sales of a specific product.

Reducing Abandoned Carts

Try to understand that your business is potentially losing money whenever a user or a visitor abandons his cart without making a purchase. Plenty of visitors can easily add items to their carts, but they tend to abandon them for various reasons before completing the checkout process. Try to address as many of the hesitations as shoppers might have. The simplest way to reduce the rate of abandoned carts is by gently reminding the visitors about their abandoned carts. Perhaps you can persuade them by offering free shipping or even a discount.

A simple yet effective e-commerce marketing idea to reduce the frequency of abandoned carts is by using email recovery campaigns. Go through the different tips discussed in the previous chapter to build an email list. Once your email list is in place, you can email them whenever you notice that the users in your list didn't complete a purchase or have abandoned their carts on your website. For instance, the email you can send such users could be along the lines of, "Did you forget something? ___ are still waiting for you in the cart!" Whatever email responses designed need to be quite enticing and should remind those juice or why he was purchasing the products in the first place.

Upselling

Upselling is an incredible tactic that has been used by marketers since forever. Upselling merely means increasing the cart value or the order value. You might have probably heard some variation of a sentence that essentially means, "Would you like to increase your cart value?" Instead of working on acquiring new customers, upselling can be quite profitable too. At times, customers are not aware of all the premium products available, or they probably need more guidance to understand how an upgraded package is better suited for their needs. For instance, if you are selling handmade leather items, then to upsell the items, you can add leather polish, brush, or even wax to increase the cart value. You can also come up with enticing combos to tempt the users to increase their overall cart value. By doing this, if a buyer who would have spent $ 20 on one purchase can end up spending $ 30 on a purchase. It might not sound like much in easily, but over a period, the amount earned from up selling will certainly add up.

There are two important considerations while you use upselling to increase the sales of your business. Ensure that the product you are upselling is directly related to or is complimentary with the original product. The second point is to be sensitive to the anticipated price range of your target audience. The product must not only fit your customer's original needs, but it needs to be within the price range that your target audience might not want to exceed.

Using Instagram

Gone are the days when social media was restricted to just Facebook. One of the most powerful and frequently used social media platforms these days is Instagram. Instagram has over 500 million daily active users. So, why shouldn't you leverage the power of the wide reach this platform offers? Using compelling photos, strategic hashtags, and publishing at the right time is a great way to build an Instagram following for your e-commerce store. The idea is to understand the importance of organic Instagram presents by increasing your engagement with the followers you have. So, it is not just about posting photos or content, but it is also about engaging with your target audience. The more you engage with them, the greater the chances that they will convert into paying customers.

Some of the simplest ways to engage with your target audience on Instagram is by running contests, going behind the scenes, or showcasing product development. Don't forget to experiment with various Instagram features like stories, IGTV, or even the different challenges that keep popping up. Keep the Instagram page light, friendly, fun, entertaining, and quirky. Don't make the content serious, brisk, and business-like. Instead, try to leverage the power of social media to increase the online visibility of your business.

Launching A Facebook Store

Facebook might not be the only social media platform available these days, but it certainly is a platform you cannot afford to overlook. The simplest way to make the most of Facebook is by launching a Facebook store. It is a great way to market your e-commerce store online. You can make sales via a Facebook store. You can also integrate this store with your Shopify store, so you don't have to maintain any separate inventory. Creating a Facebook store is a straightforward process. By placing a Facebook store tab on your business page, you can direct the users to purchase whatever products they liked directly from the Facebook profile. Instead of opening your website. The Facebook store app is an excellent and affordable way to increase your business exposure because of the large audience base that Facebook offers. Facebook stores can help increase new sales, increases the engagement potential with your customers, and belts plenty of brand awareness and recognition.

Wishlist Reminders

Don't forget to send wish list reminder emails to your subscriber list. The wish list reminder is quite similar to an email you would send an abandoned cart user. The purpose of both these emails is to convince them to shop or to nudge them toward making a purchase, instead of abandoning the cart altogether. As long as the user shows intent to buy, that is all you need to send a wish list email. Most of the online shopping apps tend to send notifications or emails in the form of wish list reminders. Is there an item on sale that's been included in several wish lists? Is the item selling out? Has it been a while since someone has reviewed their wish list? Well, if the answer is yes to all these questions, then it is time to send a quick wish list reminder. At times, users tend to forget about their carts after a while. Gently remind them, the best way to do it is by sending an email. Also, it might be the only push the user needs to become a paying customer.

Email Campaigns

In the previous chapter, you were given different tips you can follow to grow your email subscriber list. However, all those email addresses will do your business no good unless you use them effectively to market your e-commerce store. Businesses should regularly send valuable emails to all the subscribers on their email list. There are different occasions where sending an email is the ideal way to show that you appreciate your subscribers and the support they have shown towards your business. The simplest way to do this is by sending a welcome email as soon as a user makes a purchase. Don't forget to send regular newsletters alerting all your subscribers about new products, tips to use existing products, discounts, new offers, or any other news that is deemed appropriate for them. You can also use emails to send exclusive gifts or promo codes to all your subscribers. You can also share relevant content with all your customers to ensure that they make the most of their purchases. As long as the content is valuable to your target audience, don't hesitate to hit send. However, don't go overboard with all these emails. Ensure that you don't send more than one newsletter every week. If you bombard your subscribers with emails, they will quickly unsubscribe.

Avoid Poor Design

If your e-commerce store isn't well designed or is poorly designed, you will quickly lose more customers than you gain. A poorly designed site not only looks untrustworthy, but it often uses confusing navigation, offers an unclear value proposition, and uses the barely legible font. As stressed in the previous chapters, the design of your website is quintessential. When it comes to an e-commerce business. Since you don't have a physical storefront that your target audience can visit, your e-commerce store acts as the storefront. Spend sufficient time and don't rush into web designing. Shopify is an incredibly simple platform to use. As long as you're willing to dedicate the required time and effort, you can design a professional-looking website with little or no technical skills.

Keep in mind that regardless of how wonderful all the products offered on your website are, it doesn't make any sense if the users don't find your website engaging or appealing. First impressions matter a lot when it comes to online business. Therefore, make sure that the overall look of your website is pleasing and easy on the eyes.

Content Marketing

If you want to improve the ranking of your e-commerce store in search engine results or want to connect with your customers regularly, then consider blogging. If you are already churning out content, then try featuring it on a blog present on your online store. However, there are different ways in which you can do content marketing, which isn't necessarily restricted to creating a blog. You can also guest post on different websites or blogs to build awareness and create backlinks to your website. You can start a podcast featuring guest speakers. If you want, you can also create long-form content in the form of books and guides that your target audience will find helpful.

Use User-Generated Content

Generating social proof has become incredibly important in today's online world. The simplest way to do this is by using user-generated content. Whenever prospective customers view that others, just like them, are purchasing products from your website regularly, it increases their confidence in your business. One of the most effective ways to use user-generated content is by asking customers to post pictures where they are using the products you sell. For instance, if you sell clothes or shoes, you can encourage your customers to post pictures on their social media accounts wearing your products and tagging your business. It is not as customer reviews and testimonials that help improve your social proof, but even this simple tactic will work.

Personalization Matters

When it comes to increasing your online sales, personalization is a rather effective tactic. By using behavioral data, you can serve personalized experiences to all your visitors. Not a lot of businesses are aware of this tactic. So, try to make the most of it today. You can also use location to personalize or curate an experience that specifically caters to customers. Situated in a specific part of the world. For instance, if your website sells bathing suits, then ensure that you offer discounts and deals right before spring sets in. It could also happen that someone situated in Southern California might be looking for bathing suits during October, while those situated in Maine will probably look for winter wear.

Reward Loyal Customers

It is not just important to gain new customers, but you must also hold onto your loyal ones. Your loyal customers are the brand advocates you get free of charge. If you are doing a good job and have a loyal customer base, don't forget to appreciate them. Also, let them know you appreciate their continued support and association. There are various ways in which you can reward loyal customers or even big spenders by creating customer loyalty programs. You can give them extra incentives whenever they make a purchase or always give them priority access during offers running on your platform. Everyone likes to feel special and exclusive. When you give your loyal customers exclusive treatment, the chances are that they will stay loyal will increase.

Keep in mind that you're the only one that can decide how, when, and for what you wish to reward you, customers. For instance, you might come up with a point-based program on your online store, where certain points will be credited to a user's account whenever he makes a purchase. After collecting a predetermined number of points, the user can redeem them on any subsequent purchase he makes. You can also offer limited-time offers, free shipping, or other simple freebies to thank the loyal customers for their continued business.

By following the simple tips given in this chapter, you can improve the online visibility, traffic, and even sales your business makes. That said, keep in mind that it takes consistent time and effort to obtain the desired results from these marketing tactics. Learn to be patient, carefully monitor the results, and keep changing tactics according to the needs of your business.

CHAPTER EIGHT

OVERVIEW OF DROP-SHIPPING

What is Drop-Shipping?

In a regular store, you are required to invest plenty of capital, maintain inventory, and take care of different things like supply chain management. As a store owner, the responsibility of the owner always rests on your shoulders to not just receive the orders, but also fulfill them on time. However, all this can be a little scary and even overwhelming for a first-time store owner.

If you are quite excited and eager to enter the eCommerce space but are apprehensive about managing different aspects like manufacturing, order fulfillment, or supply chain management, then opt for drop-shipping. Drop-shipping is an incredibly simple form of business, and as a drop-shipper, you are effectively free from all headaches associated with inventory management. Whenever your e-commerce store receives an order, the order is directly sent to a third party or a supplier who then fulfills the order by directly shipping it to the desired customer or shopper. So, in this entire process, you don't even have to maintain a physical inventory of the products while fulfilling all the orders. So, if a customer (C) orders from your drop-shipping website (A), then the order will be forwarded to your supplier (B). The B will take care of the packing and shipping to ensure that C receives the order on A's behalf. In a regular business model, all the functions performed by B will be performed by A.

Starting a drop-shipping website is incredibly simple, especially while using an e-commerce store solution like Shopify. It will not take you more than a day or two to create the website. Once this is done, you can source all the products and then open up the store for business. In this section, you'll learn about the different steps to start a drop-shipping business on Shopify, such as finding a niche for yourself, started sourcing the products, and opening the virtual storefront.

Pros and Cons of Drop-Shipping

One of the major benefits of using drop-shipping is that it enables you to skip the burden of maintaining an inventory. Maintaining inventory is quite a hassle. It not only requires space but also needs a proper tracking system in place to maintain the overall quality of the products you offer. By allowing yourself to escape this burden, you have more time and resources available to concentrate on expanding and growing your business.

Inventory is not only a hassle to manage, but it can quickly become quite expensive. Most of the retailers usually stock up on large quantities of inventory to get the best possible price while maximizing their bottom line. However, when you pay the money upfront, it can eat into your bank balance quite easily. When it comes to drop-shipping, your business can come up with a rather productive way using all the money or cash that would have been usually set aside to acquire and maintain inventory.

When it comes to drop-shipping, all the pressure associated with maintaining and exhausting and inventory are effectively removed from the equation. So, there is plenty of pressure taken off you. If you maintain inventory and there is plenty of unsold stock leftover, then it directly translates into a loss. All this pressure can result in delays associated with changing the inventory or updating your online store. When it comes to drop-shipping, this risk is essentially eliminated to a certain degree. After all, you will only pay for what you sell.

When you remove different limitations like high overhead costs and space available, as a retailer, you are free to offer more choices to all your potential customers. Well, the customers will certainly love to choose. If you offer them a variety of products, it becomes easier to engage more customers. As long as your supplier can supply the goods, you can list as many products as you want on the drop-shipping website. Also, when you offer a variety of choices, it becomes easier to stay afloat in the dynamic and ever-changing world of sales.

Now, let us look at the different risks associated with a drop-shipping business model. The first risk is that it reduces the control you have over the entire operation. Since you no longer are in charge of the inventory shipping, a third party starts playing a major role in your business. If you don't like the idea of sharing control with others, then this business model might not work for you. If your supplier makes an error while delivering the order or leaves an unhappy customer behind, it will reflect poorly on your business. With drop-shipping, you no longer have to worry about bulk purchasing any inventory. If you don't purchase inventory in bulk, then you can effectively say goodbye to all the attractive offers. You used to get on bulk purchases. So, the cost associated with every item on your drop-shipping website might be slightly higher and will not be as competitive as you would have liked them to be.

As a drop-shipper, a benefit of drop-shipping is that your business is free to react to the customers' demands and address them accordingly. On the downside, it also suggests that you might have to deal with sudden shortages in stock. If a specific item tends to become popular overnight, you might miss out on a couple of selling opportunities because the supplier doesn't have sufficient stock to meet the demand.

Why Shopify for Drop-Shipping?

Before learning about how to start a drop-shipping store, it is important to understand your reasons to start a drop-shipping store. In this section, let us look at the reasons why using Shopify is a good idea for your drop-shipping business.

One of the major reasons to use Shopify is that it is drop-shipper friendly. This platform offers various solutions that are specially designed for a drop-shipping business model, such as Oberlo, that works brilliantly well with Shopify. Shopify is incredibly easy to use and is one of the most user-friendly platforms available in the market these days. It certainly offers a variety of features and functions, Bart, they are overwhelming, and you can easily understand what's to be done. Another important advantage of Shopify for your drop-shipping business is because of all the various features it offers. Shopify not only enables you to create an eCommerce website but also helps design and handle everything associated with the business.

Start a Drop-Shipping Business

Find a Niche

The first step to establishing a drop-shipping business is to find out what you wish to sell and outlining your target audience. So, you essentially need to find a niche before you can establish your business. There is plenty of advice available out there to understand how you can go about selecting a niche. The simplest way to do this is by carefully analyzing your passion, hobbies, and interests. Once you go through these things, you might be able to understand the right product your business can sell. Another way to look for a niche is to target products that are quite trendy and profitable.

Well, you don't have to stick to one of these ways and can use both these techniques to select a niche that you are interested in. However, while selecting the niche, ensure that it is something you are genuinely interested in. If you don't have an interest in what you're selling, you will quickly lose interest in your business. Also, it becomes difficult to convince others to become spending customers if you don't believe in what your business offers. For instance, if you are interested in yoga, maybe start your research by looking into areas like health or fitness to make a list of items you can probably sell.

There are three simple steps you can follow while finding a niche is by doing keyword research, determining the product trends, and figuring out the overall profitability. Once you are aware of the specific area of the market you want to concentrate on, look for relevant keywords.

If health or fitness is the niche, then relevant keywords could include workout clothes, gym clothes, yoga pants, yoga mats, and so on. By doing a quick keyword search, you can determine the niche. Once you obtain the keyword data, combine it with trend data to understand which item is gaining popularity. You can use simple tools such as Google trends to search and determine the product trend. The final step is to determine whether the niche is profitable. If you notice that there are too many competitors or there are no competitors in the niche, then avoid such a niche. If there are too many competitors, the cost will be quite high, while the profits can be low. On the other hand, if there are no competitors, it might mean good prices and profits.

Secure Suppliers

Your drop-shipping business cannot be a success unless you have a good supplier in place. Partnering with the wrong supplier can essentially spell disaster for your business. Therefore, thoroughly conduct the required due diligence before you select a drop-shipping supplier. Ensure that the drop-shipping supplier can respond to any product demand and fulfill all the orders on time, as promised. One of the largest online resources you can use to search, connect, and communicate with potential manufacturers and suppliers who can be used as drop-shippers is a platform such as Alibaba. Ensure that you ask plenty of questions and thoroughly vet the supplier about his production abilities before you get anyone on board.

Once you are aware of the products you wish to sell, you need to look for drop-shipping suppliers. Also, the supplier must be sure that he fits all your needs and requirements. Depending on the product, the niche you choose, and delivery times, you can choose a domestic or an overseas supplier. Once you make a list of suppliers, it is time to contact them. By talking to them, you can ask them about the services they provide and get a first-hand experience of working with them. By doing this, you have a better idea of what you're getting into. Make a list of your top three or four favorite suppliers. Once this list is in place, you can order a couple of samples from the supplier. It helps test the quality of the service, packaging, delivery time, and the overall customer experience. If you are unhappy with the customer experience, you might need to find another supplier or business. If a supplier disappoints you, then the chances are that you will end up disappointing your customers as well. If your supplier doesn't work well with your business, it will reflect poorly on your own business.

Another great way to find a supplier of yourself is by going through the products offered by your competitors. If you notice any of your competitors are using a supplier that you wish to use, then order from your competitor.

It will give you an idea about how the supplier works and whether you actually want to bring him on board or not.

While selecting a drop-shipping supplier, there are certain factors you must pay attention to reviews, feedback, and quality of products. Apart from these things, there are other red flags you must watch out for to prevent inviting a bad supplier onboard. A red flag you must watch out for is that the drops-hipping supplier insists on the payment of a monthly or an ongoing fee to conduct business with your website. Do some research and stay away from all suppliers who charge a high pre-order fee. A final aspect you must keep in mind when selecting a supplier is to go through their policies about minimum order size. Usually, suppliers charge a minimum order fee to fulfill orders. For instance, if your supplier's minimum order size is 150 units, then you need to pay upfront for the 150 units, but the supplier will fulfill the orders only when he receives them from your online store.

Name the Shopify Drop-Shipping Store

Once you are aware of your needs and have secured suppliers, it is time to name the Shopify store. Ensure that the name of the Shopify store is creative, simple, and memorable. There are various online name generator apps and tools you can use to get started with this process. Once you come up with a couple of names or ideas, check the names that are available.

Create a Shopify Account

It is time to create an account for your drops-hipping store on Shopify. The first step is to visit the homepage of Shopify, then enter your email address to get started. Once you enter the email address, you'll be required to create a password for the Shopify account and the name further drop-shipping store on Shopify. Then there are a couple of questions you must fill out about your experience with eCommerce and other personal details. Once you complete all these steps, your Shopify account will be ready for use.

Always Optimize the Shopify Account

Now that you have created a drop-shipping store, it is quite important to go through the different settings of the Shopify account. This is one step you cannot overlook if you wish to receive payments from your customers, create/policies, or even establish any shipping rates. The three aspects of your Shopify business you need to optimize are the payment information, store, policies, and shipping rates.

The first step is to add a payment option to the drop-shipping store on Shopify. It is an incredibly important step, and you cannot receive any money from your customers if you don't offer a payment option. Ensure that there are a couple of payment options available, and you are not restricting yourself to just one mode of payment. From PayPal to allowing debit or credit cards, there's plenty to choose from.

As a drop-shipping store owner on Shopify, ensure that you spend sufficient time to create the required store policies. If you are unsure of where to start, Shopify offers a helpful tool that allows you to automatically generate standardized policies for refunds, privacy, and any other terms and conditions associated with the store. To access this tool, open Shopify settings and click on the option "checkout" and scroll to the bottom of the page to find all the details. Once you find the details, click on the "generate," button and all the policies you require will be increased.

The shipping rates must be clear while establishing a Shopify drop-shipping store. The easiest option is to offer free shipping. If the shipping rates are different for different reasons, it can become incredibly confusing for your customers. So, try to incorporate the shipping prices into the final price of the product you offer and make shipping free. For instance, if it costs $5 to ship a $ 20 item, instead of charging separately for shipping, ensure that you are selling the product for $25.

Time to Launch the Drop-Ship Store

Now that you created and optimized the Shopify store for drop-shipping, it is time to launch the drop-shipping store. To launch the store, go to the "sales channels" section on the settings on your Shopify page. From there, select the option, "add an online store." Once you complete the setup, your online store will be up and running.

Design the Drop-Ship Store on Shopify

Never underestimate the importance of designing a store on Shopify. The eCommerce store design needs to be aesthetically pleasing, and it is as important as the enticing shop window of a regular brick and mortar store. As mentioned in the previous chapters, your business website or the drops-hipping website essentially acts as the first impression the user will have of your business. Therefore, it is important to make the first impression count. There are two main aspects of store design you need to consider, and they are the theme and the logo.

Shopify offers a variety of themes, and you merely need to go through them to select one that caters to your needs. Go through all the information given in the previous chapters about store design and themes to create your drop-shipping store on Shopify. If you think you don't have the skills or the expertise required to design a logo for your store, then hire a professional to do it for you. With drop-shipping, the business logo matters a lot.

Don't Forget the Drop-Shipping Apps

Drop-shipping store. Shopify, it is time to add products to the store to generate revenue. Finding products, installing an app, or a tool such as Oberlo. Go through the different Shopify apps discussed in the previous chapter to determine the best Shopify apps available. Oberlo allows you to directly and easily import different products to your drop-shipping store without any hassle and is also seamlessly integrated into Shopify. Once you have installed this application with Shopify, you can add different categories to your Shopify store. The product categories need to be based on the product of the items you wish to sell. For instance, if you want to sell T-shirts, then the product category name should be T-shirts.

Time for the First Sale

Once you have successfully completed all the different steps discussed in this section, it is time to earn revenue and make some sales using your Shopify drop-shipping store. It's highly unlikely that you'll be able to gather all the large volumes of traffic by merely launching the store on Shopify. So, you need to concentrate on different marketing tactics and come up with marketing campaigns to attract the attention of your audience. You need to have a customer acquisition plan in mind. A great product idea and website is just the start of a business. You cannot immediately obtain customers by completing these two steps. Use the different marketing tactics discussed in the previous chapters to optimize your Shopify business and online presence to gather more customers.

Now that your business is up and running, your work doesn't end here. Pick a point to constantly analyze and optimize all the metrics and data you receive to grow your business. Go through your marketing and ad campaigns to understand the ads that are networking. Redouble your efforts in the areas where you lack and try to improve yourself in the areas where you are already doing well. Make changes to your product listings and add a couple of new suppliers. Keep track of your sales, and your expenses, also. Once you do all things, you can effectively increase your chances of earning profits and growing the business.

CHAPTER NINE

OVERVIEW OF PRIVATE LABELING

What is a Private Label?

A private-label product is a product that is manufactured by another company under the brand name of some other company. From foods to cosmetics, there are a variety of industries in which you can find Private label products. When used properly, private-label items can help generate incredible profits but also handles the degree of credibility and trust you share with your customers. You might have purchased a private label product at some point, and you perhaps didn't even realize it was a private label product. It could be a bottle of jam branded with the supermarket's name you usually shop from or maybe a generic medicine available at the local chemist. In private labeling, you are essentially purchasing generic brand items, then branding them under your own label before selling them to others.

The Benefits of Private Labeling

Less Competition

If you are a private label seller, then the competition involved in any given niche will be quite low. In fact, you don't have to worry about getting overcrowded by various competitors. There will certainly be some competition, but it will be relatively less when compared to selling branded goods. After all, there are only so many discounts and offers you can give. After a point, lending customization, exclusivity, and controlling quality are the only ways in which you can do better than your competition.

Quality Control

As soon as you obtain the product, you are in complete control over what happens to the product after that. You can process it, redesign it, or even customize it to fit your needs and requirements. Therefore, you have complete control over the quality of the final product. This kind of control is not available with regular branded products. Also, if you are interested in creating your own brand, quality control is quite important. When your customers know that they can expect good quality products from you, then they will be willing to choose your private-label over other branded items available on the market.

Wholesale Income

As a private-label seller, you will mostly be required to purchase through genetics products in bulk. When you purchase in bulk, then you can get better deals. Usually, good discounts and deals are offered on all sorts of bulk purchases. Also, the costs involved in obtaining the products like shipping charges and taxes payable will reduce when you order all your supplies in a single order. You can capitalize on wholesale discounts to effectively reduce the costs of producing private-labeled products.

Better Margins

In any eCommerce store, where you and your competitors sell the same products, then you have little control over the pricing. You don't have the freedom to determine the pricing and need to make your prices competitive. When it comes to private-label products, there's plenty of freedom. Your competitors might be required to sell an existing brand product for a specific price, whereas you have the choice to customize the price at which you wish to sell. For instance, a specific pair of branded shoes cannot be sold below or above a market price established by the said brand. Now, with private labeling, you are free to determine the price level.

Boosting Compensation

The profit margin is relatively higher in private label products, and you can use this to increase your sales. When your profit margin is higher, then you can use the excess funds to boost compensations to tempt your target audience to become paying customers. The competition margin on private-label products is relatively high. Therefore, you will end up saving plenty even after taking care of all the business expenses.

Build a Brand

Private labeling enables you to start your own brand online. For instance, if you are a fashion store, you can sell products related to fashion like clothes, shoes, bags, or even accessories. You can sell all these under your own brand name. To do this, the first step is to order the products from other manufacturers without any labels, then attach your label to them before selling them to the store. You can also procure generic products and then customize them to fit your brand image before selling them online. You have the flexibility required to design, create, or even curate the required modifications to the generic products before making them available for sale.

Increased Loyalty

With the increase in demand for exclusivity these days, the more exclusive a product seems, the higher is its demand. So, private-label products offer a certain degree of exclusivity because you're the only one who will be producing a specific type of product. Therefore, it is quintessential that you pay attention to the kind of product you wish to sell. Also, keep in mind that people favor locally made products rather than mass-produced generic goods. If you're the only source they can obtain products from; then it makes you seem like an expert in the niche.

The Risks of Private Labeling

As with everything else in the world, there are certain risks involved with private labeling as well. However, if you plan and take certain strategic decisions, you can quickly avoid or overcome any of the risks involved. In this section, let us look at some of the potential risks of private labeling.

Order Values

One of the major drawbacks of opting for private labeling is that most manufacturers ask for a minimum order. This minimum order limit is usually quite high, and you cannot place an order unless you meet this limit. For instance, if your business idea is to sell printed t-shirts, then the supplier or manufacturer might have a minimum order limit of 200 t-shirts. So, unless you place the order for at least 200 t-shirts, the manufacturer will not supply the t-shirts you need. The simplest way to overcome this problem is to negotiate with the seller or the vendor. Otherwise, you can also try and convince them to provide the same product in various shapes and sizes to meet the minimum order requirement.

General Perception

Trusting private-label products does take a certain degree of faith. For instance, if you're at a local supermarket and you see certain products marketed under the supermarket's name, then you have the option of testing and seeing the products they sell. Maybe the local supermarket is selling a bottle of ketchup under its own name. Since you're at a physical store, you can go, look at the product, see how it looks, and then purchase it. With online businesses, customers don't have the luxury of seeing the products physically before making a purchase and merely need to trust what the product description says.

There also exists a popular misconception that branded products are of higher quality, whereas private-label products are of inferior quality. Therefore, ensure that you conduct a thorough research about your target audience before you invest in any private-label products. Understand your target audience, their likes, and dislikes, those references, and come up with a list of qualities that need to be present in your private labeled product. Ensure that the product you have branded is comparable with other similar products on the market.

Dead Inventory

At times, eCommerce store owners tend to make the wrong choice and order certain products for private labeling without understanding whether they will appeal to the target audience or not. In such a case, you might end up with excess inventory that you cannot sell due to the lack of demand. With branded products, you can easily return them and get a refund for any investment you make. However, the private-label products, generic products are rebranded, and therefore, it becomes increasingly difficult to resell them. Dealing with dead inventory is one aspect of the business you can easily overcome, and this is by doing thorough product research. Before you can procure any supplies, ensure that there is sufficient demand in the market for the product you wish to sell. If there is no demand, then stay away from such a niche.

Steps to Start a Private Labeling Business

Pick a Niche

Regardless of what you do, the one thing you must never do is start a business you are not passionate about. Therefore, it is quite essential to understand what works and doesn't work for you. Keep in mind that every person is different. What might work for one person doesn't necessarily have to work for you. As a private-label seller, you are essentially trying to reinvent an existing product or market a brand-new product to your existing audience. So, what is the best product you can choose for private labeling? Well, as with a business idea, the product you choose must also belong to the niche or an industry that interests you. If you're just getting started with private labeling, you can probably think of a hobby you enjoy where you purchased a low-priced item.

For instance, if you are interested in fashion, you can sell customized t-shirts on Shopify. Pick up a couple of generic t-shirts and jazz them up with prints, designs, or even bedazzle them! These simple practices can help transform a basic generic product into a branded item that can be sold on Shopify.

Another simple way to understand the niche you wish to target is by leveraging the power of search engines. The main advantage of using search engines is the sheer volume they can provide. Most of the marketplace search engines work by promoting specific items that sell the most for a particular phrase or word. Try to target these keywords; you can quickly come up with a list of products that are doing exceptionally well in the market.

Work With Your Passion or Interest

When it comes to building an online business or an eCommerce store, always choose something you're passionate about. If you carefully go through the success stories of incredibly successful people, you will realize that they manage to be successful because they follow a passion. If you're not passionate about your business, you'll quickly lose interest in it. Also, the chances of giving up increased significantly, especially when faced with obstacles. Staying in business requires plenty of resilience. Unless you are passionate about your business, you will not find the resilience of the motivation required to keep going or standing ground.

You can go through various marketing strategies, product ideas, and business ideas, but all these things will not make any sense if they are not in sync with your passion. Always stay true to yourself. When it comes to earning money online, there isn't a straightforward strategy that can be used by everyone. Any strategy that you deal with needs to be refined according to your lifestyle and interests. Just because you notice something works for one person doesn't mean it will work well for your business.

Search for Opportunities

As an eCommerce store owner, you are an entrepreneur, before anything else. As an entrepreneur, you should be adept at spotting opportunities or carving out opportunities in business. As a private-label seller, most of the money you earn will be from items that already have a busy time on the market. Ensure that you search for high-volume keywords with low competition and base your choices on that opportunity.

The simplest way to look for opportunities is to browse through various selling platforms you would want to use for your business. You can do this in different ways. The simplest way to go about doing this is to cross-reference all the different marketplaces that you can sell as a private-label. From Amazon to eBay, or even Shopify, see how hard it would be to start your Shopify store based on the competition present in the niche associated with the keywords you have chosen. The simplest way to understand whether someone cares about a product or not is by going through the reviews. If a specific product has tons of reviews, you can assume that the product is doing fairly well on the market and has considerable demand too.

Understand the Margins

As a private-label seller or a private-label business on Shopify, keep in mind that your aim must be to double the money on every product and sale you make. It is the best way to ensure that your business stays profitable. As soon as you select a product for private labeling, add the costs incurred to rebrand, back, and ship the product. For instance, if the generic T-shirt you wish to private-label costs $5, then add other costs incurred to redesign, bedazzle, or even print the t-shirt. Don't forget to add the fees payable to the hosting platform like Shopify while doing this. So, the end product might end up costing $10. Once you have this figure, add the desirable profit margin to it, and the final sum will be the total selling price.

Meet Manufacturers

Once you have identified a business idea, niche, a product type that you think will work well. Fear private-label, the next step is to meet the manufacturers. If you don't find a manufacturer for the generic product, you cannot start private labeling it immediately. There are a couple of simple ways in which you can find a manufacturer for your private-label business. The simplest way is to run a Google search. While using Google to search, ensure that the keywords you use are super-specific. Even a simple search like "T-shirt manufacturers (chosen area)" will give you surprisingly good hits on Google. Another way to go about doing this is to check wholesale websites like Alibaba. If you can source the product at extremely low prices, then it reduces the overheads while giving you a chance to increase your profit share.

Once you made a list of all the potential manufacturers that you want to do business with, it is time to order some supplies from them. Before you decide to bring a manufacturer on board, order samples from them- if the samples arrive on time, are of the right quality, and within your budget, then you can shortlist all the manufacturers.

Select the Right Manufacturer

While choosing a product manufacturer, ensure that he is someone who cares about the business and would want to do business with you. Also, be mindful of various companies out there that are merely created with the intent of scamming others. If the other person is not willing to use an escrow service of some type, such as PayPal, never indulge in any transactions. Spend some time, do your due diligence before bringing any manufacturer on board. Also, be mindful of all those manufacturers who demand a certain fee to be paid every month. The same steps that you followed while selecting a supplier for the drop-shipping business are applicable to finding the right manufacturer for private labeling.

Marketing a Private Label Product

You need to market private-label products. Regardless of how wonderful and truly great the product is, you will not have any bio long as they are available about the products you have to offer. So, how can you market a private-label product? The simplest way to get started is to inform your contact list about what you do and your business. After this, it is time to make the most of your social media accounts. Post videos and pictures about your products, inform your followers about all that you offer and share links to your Shopify website. Never underestimate the power of social media marketing. Follow the different tips discussed in the previous section about marketing your Shopify store to increase the visibility of your private-label product.

Showcase the Products

Once you have everything else in place, it is time to showcase your private-label. After all, if you don't showcase these items, you cannot earn any revenue from them. The best place to showcase private-label products is Shopify. Follow the different steps given in the previous chapters to create and launch the Shopify store. Once you have completed all the steps, you merely need to add the private-label products you wish to sell to the Shopify store. After you do all this, the Shopify store is up and ready for business. Use every channel you can possibly think of to grow and improve your Shopify store and business. Try to build as much awareness about your private-label product as you possibly can.

While dealing with private label products on Shopify, you have a unique opportunity to grow yourself as an entrepreneur. One thing you must never stop is learning all that you can about private labels. Knowledge is power when it comes to any form of business. If you want to stay ahead of the game, then ensure that you are always informed.

CHAPTER TEN

MISTAKES TO AVOID

Are you just getting started with an eCommerce business? At times, the entire process can be a little overwhelming, and creating your first venture will seem like a daunting task. However, with practice, it will all get easier. Making mistakes is an elementary aspect of learning. Well, you don't necessarily have to make mistakes to learn. You can learn a lot from the mistakes of others too. In this section, let us look at some of the most common Shopify mistakes and how to avoid them.

Using the Default Settings

Concentrating on SEO should be your priority if you want to increase the visibility of your online store or the products you offer. To increase your SEO ratings, avoid using the default settings for Meta tags. So, every page, blog post, and product must be inserted manually into the Meta tags for your website's SEO. Whenever you edit a product or a page, open the Edit Website SEO option at the bottom of the page and then click on the edit Meta Information. If you fail to do this, then the first 160 characters from your webpage, collection, or product page will be set as the default title. SEO is not just important to improve your online visibility, but also offers a better user experience.

Lack of a Uniform Theme

All the different colors present in the Shopify theme must match your store. Therefore, always double-check the color consistency. For instance, any clickable links to your website must be of the same color. Carefully go through the different configurations and website settings to ensure that all the vital information is displayed consistently. To create a consistent shopping experience for all your customers, carefully review the selections of your eCommerce store.

No Branding

The image of your business in the market is conveyed through its logo. Even if your eCommerce store is launched on a wide scale, your brand might not amass a huge following, if it doesn't have a logo. What is the first thing that comes to your mind when you view a bright yellow M? You might be reminded of McDonald's. So, never underestimate the power of branding, and always have a logo to create quick business recognition. If you don't think you have the required skills to design the logo, don't hesitate to hire some professional help.

Improper Contact Information

The about us or the contact page is quite important for any eCommerce store or website. It is one page you cannot afford to overlook if you want to be a successful eCommerce store owner. The About Us page is your business's primary introduction to its potential customers. This page talks about the vision, mission, and value statement of your business and its unique selling point. It must also include contact information like phone number, email, actress, fax number, and a PO box address wherever applicable.

Checkout Page Matters

There are many customization options available for checkout pages on Shopify. Therefore, always check the checkout pages of the website before you launch the store. When you use the website or the e-commerce store from a customer's perspective, you will get a better insight into the things that work and don't work in your favor. It is quintessential that the checkout process on your e-commerce store is easy and hassle-free. Ideally, the look of the checkout page must be similar to the other pages of your e-commerce store. Also, ensure that the font used is similar throughout the website. The checkout page should not seem like a misplaced extension of your eCommerce Shopify store.

Limit the Font Selection

Shopify offers a variety of fonts, and finding the right kind of font for your eCommerce store might seem a little daunting. Before you select a font, always shortlist at least two or three fonts and then find one that fits well with your brand and store name. You can create a variety of looks using a single font type due to the various options available, like bold, letter spacing, thin, italics, and regular styles. If you want to lend a polished and well-defined look to your eCommerce store, then the font style needs to be consistent across the website. You cannot use one font style for a page and then change it for the other pages. Also, if you use multiple fonts on a single page, it makes the website seem cluttered.

Don't Overlook the Soft Launch

Before you line up for a grand online opening, opt for a soft launch of the online store. In a soft launch, introduce your website or eCommerce store only to a limited number of people. Before this site goes live for everyone, conduct a soft launch. When you do this, you will get a rough idea about the different features of your site that work and don't work in its favor. Use the feedback you receive from a soft launch, and you can make any required changes before the website goes live. A soft launch is like a select screening of a movie before its actual release.

Not Offering Multiple Payment Options

If you want to increase the value of sales and the number of customers your online store gathers, then you need to offer a variety of payment options. Never restrict yourself to a single payment gateway and include a couple of options. If you end up offering only one or two payment options, not all your potential customers need to use the same payment gateways.

Lack of a Marketing Plan

You cannot make the most of the benefits offered by Shopify unless you have a sound marketing strategy in place. It helps provide guidelines about your target audience, selling tactics, business coach, or even the promotional setup. A good marketing plan provides a detailed overview of not just your ideal target audience but the selling cycle too. A simple way to piece together a marketing strategy is to define your brand's message and the USP, your target audience, various marketing tactics, and the different goals you have in mind.

Lack of Optimization

The landing pages are quite different from the usual pages on your business website. A landing page serves a specific purpose. The purpose is defined by the source that leads your target audience to the website. Usually, a Landing Page helps generate leads and boost a specific call to action while providing more information about the product, service offered, and any item that is sold.

Your landing pages need to be thoroughly optimized, must direct the user in the right direction, and needs to perform a specific action. An ideal landing page must guide you, visitors, capture necessary email addresses, cross-sell, or even upsell, and generate some interest in whatever your business offers.

Overlooking First-Time Visitors

Never underestimate the power of a good first impression. First impressions matter a lot, especially when it comes to selling and online selling, in particular. One mistake you must try to avoid at all costs is not putting your best foot forward while welcoming a first-time visitor to your eCommerce store. The first impression your store manages to make with them will determine whether they will proceed and make a sale or exit the website. A couple of factors you can consider to create a powerful first impression is the message your landing page of the website provides, the color scheme, the pop-ups you use, and your engagement tactics. If your website is attractive, makes the visitor feel valued, or offers very valuable information and deals, the chances of conversion will increase.

Lack of Awareness

You cannot become a successful business owner if you are unsure of your target audience. Before you think about launching your business, spend some time to answer the question, who is my target audience carefully? Regardless of how wonderful your idea is, you cannot successfully sell it if there are no takers. Therefore, you must be thoroughly aware of your ideal customer. An ideal customer is a person who is most likely to grab any product or service your website offers. When you have sufficient clarity about your target audience, it helps you select the right products and concentrate on a personalized and customized marketing strategy.

Avoid PPC Ads

Pay per click or PPC ads are an incredible way to generate more leads and increase conversions. However, plenty of people tend to overlook or underestimate the overall power PPC ads offer. It doesn't take much time or effort to launch a successful PPC campaign. If you are in it for the long run, then you cannot overlook the importance of PPC ad campaigns. A PPC campaign enables you to generate traffic and leads more quickly than organic SEO traffic. It also helps you check and change the ad budget, depending on the ROI. When your PPC campaign is well planned, you can reduce the cost per click. Also, you can use a PPC ad for A/B testing and shutdown a campaign when you don't get the desired results.

You need plenty of knowledge and understanding before you can launch a successful PPC ad campaign. If you're just getting started with Shopify, there are a couple of apps you can use to integrate PPC ad campaigns with your eCommerce store. The most popular options include Google ads and Google shopping. You can also use adNabu or other third-party apps to create and integrate a PPC ad campaign with your eCommerce Shopify story.

Ignoring Accounting

The importance of accounting can never be overlooked. Keep in mind that you are starting a business, and, as with any other business, keeping track of your accounts matters a lot. Bookkeeping, taxes, invoicing, and keeping track of expenses matter a lot. If you don't have a proper record of all this, then you might end up over or underestimating the profits you make. Also, to stay on top of all the taxes payable, you need to have solid accounts in place. If you don't want to run into any legal hassle, then never overlook the importance of detailed accounting. There are various online and accounting automation apps and software you can use to keep track of all the accounts. If you want, you can go the old school route and maintain the accounts in a journal. If you don't have the knack for accounting, then you can hire a professional to help you with all this.

CHAPTER ELEVEN

SHOPIFY TIPS FOR BEGINNERS

In this section, let's look at some incredibly simple tips you can use to make the most of your Shopify store while increasing your overall profitability.

Various Payment Options

As an eCommerce store owner or a business owner, for that matter, the payment gateway is one of the most crucial things to think about. After all, the main purpose of starting a store is to honor profit. There isn't a right or wrong way to go about selecting payment options. As long as you provide sufficient payment options and keep things streamlined, you're nothing to worry about. A simple trick you can use to retain your customers is to allow them to save their payment information by creating a profile on your website. Don't forget to offer a couple of different payment options such as debit or credit cards, bank transfers, PayPal, or even cryptocurrency.

Don't Shy Away from Social Media

The simplest way to direct more traffic towards your online store is to use the power of social media. There are various forms of paid advertising events. You can use it to achieve this goal, too. However, don't shy away from social media. There are various platforms that you can use depending upon the ones most frequently used by your target audience, and you can spread the word about your business.

Start a Blog

If you don't have a huge budget for advertising, you can concentrate on generating organic traffic to your business to offer relevant content. You can write a blog associated with your eCommerce store on Shopify. The blog needs to be packed with various helpful, entertaining, and interesting articles neatly packed with SEO keywords to increase your online visibility. A blog is a tool that not only allows you to connect with your target audience but allows them to show that there exists a real human being behind the eCommerce store. Once the most popular SEO tools you can use is the Google keyword planner.

Concentrate on SEO

Your website's ranking and performance are quite important when it comes to generating traffic to your Shopify store. To increase your website's ranking in the search engine's results, there must be plenty of relevant keywords included in the content available on your website. For instance, if you sell dog cameras and mention information about scuba diving suits on your website's main page, it will not help improve your online visibility concerning people looking for dog cameras. The content on the website must be in sync with the product or service you offer.

Mobile Optimization

These days, a significant portion of online shoppers are using the mobile phone to make purchases. Therefore, it isn't surprising that plenty of people are stepping away from their laptops and desktops and instead of using the mobile phone to access websites or apps of different stores. So, if you are starting an online store on Shopify intending to increase your sales, ensure that you come up with a mobile application for the same. If you don't want to develop a mobile app right away, ensure that the official website of the eCommerce store is thoroughly optimized to view it on a mobile phone. So, before you start to launch the website, ensure that it works well on a variety of devices, such as the desktop, mobile phone, and tablets.

Free Shipping Works

The term free shipping seems quite attractive and will look like an incredible offer too. Plenty of people are put off when they realize that they need to pay a further order to be shipped to them. Therefore, try to offer free shipping whenever possible. You can set up a minimum cart value that qualifies customers for free shipping. Another sneaky alternative is to ensure that your shipping charges are already included in the price of the item. As long as you recover all the costs incurred to create the final product, you've nothing to worry about.

Monitor your Competition

Did you ever look at the menus of Burger King and McDonald's? If you pay a little attention, you'll realize that most of the items on both the menus are quite similar. If one fast-food chain introduces a new item to the menu, the other one follows suit. Likewise, monitoring your competition is an important aspect of doing business. Regardless of whether it is online or offline. So, pay attention to your competition. Look at their business website, the products you offer, and even the suppliers you use. It not only gives your inspiration but also gives you a better idea of all the things you can do differently. If you like something that your competitor does, you can improve upon it and make your eCommerce store look more appealing. As a business owner, your primary goal must be to earn profits and stand out from the rest of the competition in the market.

High-Quality Images

Don't use stock photos for your eCommerce store on Shopify. Ensure that all the images you use are of high quality. Using poor quality, underlit, or grainy images will do your online business no favors whatsoever. Invest some time to take some high-quality product photos. Take the photos from a similar angle, use a consistent background, and keen to make your website look more appealing and aesthetically pleasing. As an eCommerce store, the product images you upload will pretty much act as the reference point for all your potential customers. To ensure that they get the most out of the experience, the product pictures need to be of good quality.

Offer Customer Support

Keep in mind that customer support is quite important for all types of businesses, and online stores are not an exception. Ensure that the information you included in the About Us and Contact Us pages are true and fair. The customer support you have in place matters a lot when it comes to ensuring that your customers have a good overall experience.

CONCLUSION

We live in a world of technology and digital media. Gone are the days when business was restricted to just physical stores. With the invention of the Internet, the world has become a global village. You don't have to worry about investing in expensive real estate or hiring a team of professionals to launch a business. All you need is a good idea and an Internet connection. It has never been this easy to launch an eCommerce business or website. All you need to do is leverage the reach and convenience of Shopify; you can quickly create a business website for yourself.

Shopify is one of the best e-commerce hosting services available in the market these days. Its popularity is steadily increasing, and it houses tens of thousands of entrepreneurs. If you believe in your idea and have secured a good product, then all that's left for you to do is to get started. If you are interested in creating an e-commerce store, then congratulations are in order! You have made it this far, so don't forget to congratulate yourself! Once you are certain about your goal, the next step is to work on turning your goal into a reality.

This book will guide you through the different steps you must follow to create your Shopify store. In this book, you were given all the information you needed to create and launch an eCommerce store on Shopify. From the different benefits Shopify offers to select a product you want to sell and steps to design the website, this book has all the information you need. You were also given information about using drop-shipping and private labeling to sell products using a Shopify eCommerce store. Apart from all this, you were given tips for marketing your Shopify store, mistakes to avoid, and simple steps every beginner can use to get started in the right direction.

Now that you are armed with all the information you require, the next step is to get started. Unless you put all the knowledge you are required to practice; you will never know. So, take the first step today and create your Shopify store immediately. Keep in mind that it takes plenty of time, effort, consistency, and patience to create an extremely profitable store on Shopify. However, if you can be resilient and show all the other characteristics, then you will become a successful business owner.

So, what are you waiting for? There is no time like the present to get started.